What the Fuck is Wrong with Me?

And What Do I Do About It?

Melanie Torkington BSW

Names, characters, places, and incidents either are the product of the author's imagination or are used fictitiously. Any resemblance to actual persons, living or dead, events, or locales is entirely coincidental.

Copyright © 2024 by Melanie Torkington

All rights reserved. No part of this book may be reproduced or used in any manner without written permission of the copyright owner except for the use of quotations in a book review. For more information, address: TimeandSpaceTherapy@gmail.com.

First paperback edition June 2024

ISBN 978-0-473-71802-2 (paperback)

ISBN 978-0-473-71845-9 (Hardcopy)

ISBN 978-0-473-71803-9 (ebook)

ISBN 978-0-473-71804-6 (Kindle)

www.TimeandSpaceTherapy.Org

*Dedicated to
Bethany Angel, Kobe Max, and Gabriella Rain*

If you ever find yourself questioning what is wrong with you, in this sometimes merciless world, I hope you hear Mumma's voice say, "You are the most magical thing I have ever known".

Contents

Safety first	6
Preface	**8**
Introduction	10
1. What the Fuck is Wrong With Me?	**14**
2. The Window of Tolerance	**17**
3. Looking at the Window	**20**
Figure 1. The basics	*21*
Figure 2. Introducing Resiliency Factors	27
The Power of Analogy	28
Figure 3. Ocean Analogy	*30*
Activity. 1 - Draw Your Own Window	33
4. Looking Through the Window: Life Examples	**35**
The Ideal	35
Escalation / De-escalation	37
Above, Below, and Back Again	40
Side note: Abuse of power	45
5. Getting to Know Your Window	**47**
Factors	47
Activity. 2 - My Factors	48
The Check-In	53
Activity. 3 - Checking In	54
Accentuating the positive	60
Toxic Positivity	61
6. Functioning and the BIG Factors	**63**
Brain and Body Functioning	64
Drugs and Substances	67
Trauma, Grief and ACEs	70

    Big Factors Need Big Solutions   76

7. House of Many Windows   79

    Activity. 4 - Your House of Windows   86

8. Out of the Window   88

    Survival Mode   88

        Fight   89

        Flight   91

        Freeze   93

        Fawn   96

    Below Zero: Flat Lining   98

    No Window of Tolerance?   101

        Figure 4. When you don't have a Window of Tolerance   101

    Behaviors: What are yours?   104

        Activity. 5 - What do I do? What can I do?   104

9. Climbing Back in the Window   109

    Resistance or Self-Preservation   110

    Mindfulness and Body   113

    De-escalation - First Aid   114

    Addressing your Factors   117

        Activity. 6 - Factors: Address or Mitigate   117

    Building Resiliency   120

        Activity. 7 - Your Resiliency Factors   121

10. How to Stay in Your Window   126

    When 'Tools' Become Resilience   126

    Boundaries   128

    What the Fuck is Right With Me?   131

        Activity. 8 - Light It Up   132

11. Conclusion   137

Safety first

Be sure to look after yourself throughout the reading of this book. If any content or activities in this book trigger you and you feel suicidal or unsafe, please call the helpline services relative to your country and seek the appropriate professional help. None of the advice, information, insights, activities, or anything in this book, is designed to replace or replicate medical or professional help where needed. Although a certain level of thought, emotion, and memory-provoking, reflection is expected with any self-development, be gentle with yourself and apply self-care and commonsense while you read this, or any book.

Window

win·dow ˈwin-(ˌ)dō

Synonyms of *Window*

1

    a: an opening for admission of light and air
    b: a space
    d: a means of entrance or access
    especially: a means of obtaining information
    c: an area enveloped by framework
    d: the framework that closes in a Window opening

2

    a: a range of wavelengths in the electromagnetic spectrum

3

    a: an interval of time
    b: an interval of time or space during which certain conditions or an opportunity exists
    a *Window* of vulnerability

4

    a: an area at the limits of the earth's sensible atmosphere

  adjective
Phrases

out the Window
: out of existence, use, or consideration.

Preface

A friend called in for coffee, flustered, looking only mildly more presentable than a bag of shit. "Mel!" She exclaimed "What the fuck is wrong with me?!" This usually calm, bubbly, lighthearted woman then went on to list her complaints and stresses at length, all after the precursor that she had given up smoking.

We had a little chat, ok, a big chat… a big deep hearty yarn, about all the things that she'd never really dealt with in her life, that were now coming to the surface. Things that were now 'allowed' to surface since the subduing effects of the nicotine, were no longer active in her system; Since the soothing 'behavior' of the smoking, no longer kept a lid on it all. She was overwhelmed by the onslaught of old feelings, new triggers, raw emotions, and all without her main coping mechanism of dealing with it. But after we talked about it all, acknowledged what was going on, she had a big release of emotion and a cuddle and off she went. The next time I saw her she felt so much better.

This poor little sweetheart, like so many people that come to see me professionally, really thought she was losing her mind. She had no idea what was wrong with

Preface

her. Yet it is the exact same thing that is often wrong with the rest of us in these moments, a build up of pressure within our system, from 'stuff' we have never addressed or dealt with in our lives.

I hate to admit it but about two months later I did the same thing to her and she made me talk about the hard stuff and cry, and god damn that woman, it was just what i needed. Because we ALL have old unresolved shit of some sort, and when you sweep enough of it under the rug, pretty soon you're going to run out of room between you and the ceiling. Then what happens? Then what do you do?

Introduction

I present "What the Fuck is Wrong With Me?", a simple framework for understanding the complexity of how fucked up you are, and what you can do about it. Being a Therapist, Social Worker, Mother, student of life, and child born into a world-of-fuckery myself, I am all too aware of the sometimes silent whisper this questioning presents throughout humankind. In a mission to empower people to answer this pondering for themselves, I offer a unique self-therapy handbook, that makes the foundational benefits of professional therapy more appealing and accessible to real-life people, everywhere. No matter who you are, or how you feel at this moment, this book will equip you with a better understanding of yourself and others. It will aid you in doing whatever decluttering of emotional closets is necessary, to enjoy increasing levels of health and happiness, then amplifying this in abundance. When things do turn to shit, it will guide you to navigate the storms of life and provide a framework for you to hang on to — giving a solid structure, to start climbing your way back into the 'window' again, finding comfort and calm.

Life is a lot of things, but one thing it is not is a never-ending stroll in the park. Things can happen that

Introduction

turn blue skies into a rough sea, with you hanging on for dear life. It's a journey filled with highs and lows, twists and turns, moments of joy, and periods of struggle. Along this path, we often encounter situations beyond our control, pushing our comfort zones, testing our resilience, and stretching our capacity to cope. In these moments, understanding and harnessing the power of our "Window of Tolerance " can be the key to riding those waves with ease.

Using the skills in this book, we learn to 'Check-In' with ourselves and curiously inquire where we haven't before. We begin to develop a visual resource that anyone can use to both assess and address their own mental/emotional state and provide their own self-therapy. It is an invitation to 'get over yourself', relax your expectations of yourself, and approach your healing with a child-like, humourous fascination, enlightening the journey and making it one of adventure and learning, instead of dread or shame.

This handbook is designed to help you find balance within your Window of Tolerance and find equilibrium. It offers practical tools and strategies to expand your Window of Tolerance, enhance emotional regulation, and build greater resilience in the face of adversity.

Introduction

Drawing upon principles from psychology, neuroscience, and mindfulness, "What the Fuck is Wrong With Me?" will guide you in:

- Understanding the dynamics of the Window of Tolerance and how to use it to both assess and address stressors in your life.
- Recognizing signs of when you or others are moving out of your coping 'window' and developing strategies to return to a state of balance.
- Building resilience and fostering a sense of inner strength to thrive in the face of adversity.
- Strategizing to change undesirable behaviors and cultivating healthy habits, thus sustaining new happier, more fulfilling lifestyles.
- Decluttering your emotional 'closet' to allow more capacity for love and joy.

Not only will it give you these skills to understand and manage yourself, it will also help you to understand others and how they may be affected by their placement within their window. This is a vital tool for all relationships, being more aware of why someone may behave the way they do and what their needs from you might be at that time.

Introduction

Once we can easily conceptualize the emotional and mental functioning of humankind in general, a whole new perspective of ourselves, our past, other people, and the world around us, is possible. One where we can easily see patterns weaving through our lifespan; where we are, where we have come from, and where we are heading, in one simple snapshot. We can then more easily see the steps forward, to a path where we are in more control, where we can be the decision maker of our future, not the situations that have programmed us in the past.

Ultimately, the following is a tale of your own self-invention. A re-writing of your story. A process that promises to challenge, inspire, and transform your relationship with yourself and the world around you. It's time to step into that power, embrace life's challenges with courage and resilience, and discover the inner guidance that lies within you. Are you ready to figure out what the fuck is wrong with you and what to do about it? Let's begin.

1. What the Fuck is Wrong With Me?

As a therapist of 15 years, "What the fuck is wrong with me?" is loosely the sentiment of what many clients are asking when they arrive at their first session. They don't always frame it like this, initially, it's delivered as a list of complaints about their life. Sometimes it starts with "What the fuck is wrong with (someone else)?" and then through implementing many of the reflections in this book, they can take their power back and work on what is within their control i.e. 'what the fuck is wrong with themselves' and what THEY can do about it.

People may present with pressures they cannot keep up with, relationships that are struggling, and behaviors that are causing them or their loved ones pain and heartbreak. It may be that they have physical ailments with no explanation, nightmares, intrusive thoughts, self-sabotage, inability to reach goals or finish projects/tasks. Some may have no idea about where any of this came from or why it showed up.

What the Fuck is Wrong With Me?

Then there are the clients who are just about screaming this question very directly, lost from even the complaints that may be contributing, they are plagued with unshakable sadness, deep-seated feelings of isolation, fear, hopelessness, anxiety, phobia, apathy, or even suicidal ideation. All of these clients, having already tried with all the willpower they previously possessed, are now reaching out with an underlying questioning "What the fuck is wrong with me?!". Which usually sits just above the surface of the core belief "I am not good enough".

This question comes from a desperate hope to find a solution; A cure for our 'not good enoughness'. Then we will finally be good enough, like everyone else, and no longer have to feel the pain of this inadequacy. It is the cry of the inner child who once internalized everything that happened around them as being attributed to their own worthiness or value. And if it was good, that meant they were good, if it was not, it was somehow because they were not good enough.

So let's cut to the chase, there's nothing wrong with you. You are as wondrous and beautiful as any other human that walked this earth. You are as perfectly organic and growing and evolving as the most divine rose in morning dew and as important as every little ray of sunshine on the face of our otherwise uninhabitable planet. You are part of a whole that needs you. You belong to the greater universe and you, as a singular being, are MORE than good enough.

You always have been.

2. The Window of Tolerance

This guide mainly utilizes 'my take' on a framework called 'The Window of Tolerance', to demonstrate what the fuck is wrong with you and with this understanding, lead to how you may be able to 'unfuck' yourself….(in staying with this blunt terminology). I also integrate a little 'Solution Focused Therapy' and a few other approaches into my work here, so if you're familiar with the traditional versions you may notice some blending.

The Window of Tolerance refers to the optimal state of 'arousal' or 'being' where we can effectively cope with stressors and engage with life's demands calmly and rationally. In this place, we are better able to experience a sense of happiness, fulfillment, clarity, and stability. Living in this zone provides the best attributes for a healthy lifestyle in almost every way.

In this ideal place, our nervous system is more regulated. We are more present in the moment. We are in touch with our emotions, our surroundings, and our intuition (wise mind or inner guidance). We function more out of a sense of faith instead of fear. We think more positively, and optimistically and these thoughts and feelings spiral to more of the same; positive, optimistic experiences. We have a greater capacity for connection because we aren't walling off from people out of distrust and fear, yet we are also in touch with our instincts and so know when to implement boundaries. We know our worth and don't hesitate to draw a line with behavior that doesn't align with it. We are in an optimum state for functioning all round.

However, life's challenges can often push us beyond this window, leading to states of hyperarousal (such as anxiety, anger, or overwhelm) or hypoarousal (such as numbness, dissociation, or shutdown). We can become accustomed to living in these 'outer states', to the point we forget that there is even an option for us. We can forget there is a whole spectrum we can exist in. Where we can live within this 'scale of coping', aka the 'Window of Tolerance', and enjoy all the benefits of a healthier, more holistically balanced life.

First coined by Dan Siegel in his 1999 book, 'The Developing Mind', The Window of Tolerance is a favorite framework of mine because it is non-prescriptive, meaning it applies to everyone. Everyone has different contributing factors to where they are on theirs, different behaviors they 'go to' when pushed outside of where they can no longer

The Window of Tolerance

'tolerate', and even different size windows, but a window they will have.

I have used this approach in different ways, to great epiphany and success, with teens, children, adults, couples, and families. I've used it to help parents understand their teens, for teens to understand their parents, for professional teams, mediation, and probably a heap in my personal life too….(without others knowing because Therapists still want to keep their friends…and friends don't always want to be 'therapised').

I'd say we are ALL able to empathize with being outside of our window at some point in our lives. Receiving some bad news, or having learned about the passing of a loved one, and having gone from totally fine; within the comfort of our Window of Tolerance, to almost immediately completely outside of it, feeling devastated, lost, frozen, or unable to function within seconds. We may have specific triggers, that to others have no effect at all, but to us, can send us from 'Zero to One Hundred' instantly, shooting out the top of our window, potentially into a defensive rage.

Whoever you are and wherever you are on the 'Window of Tolerance' at this moment, the exploration of the following concepts and tools will help you to understand yourself and others and assist you in getting the best out of all.

3. Looking at the Window

To completely understand the Window of Tolerance we need to see it in visual action. The visual reference of this framework is what makes it such a strong tool for self-reflection and monitoring. If you can imagine exactly where within the window you are at each moment of each day, you can then use it to unpack whatever is contributing to that place and if necessary, mitigate it with some tools and self-care strategies (that we'll discuss later). Sometimes just the awareness of these factors is enough to generate some gentle self-acceptance and create a safer, cozier, space within the window, bringing you further away from the edge.

The following image is the basis of everything we discuss from here on in. Study it and let the concept of it, become a well-embedded construct within your mind. Refer back to it visually at this page as much as needed, throughout the work. Bookmark it ideally. Eventually, you will see it clearly in your mind and refer to it there.

Looking at the Window

Figure 1. The basics

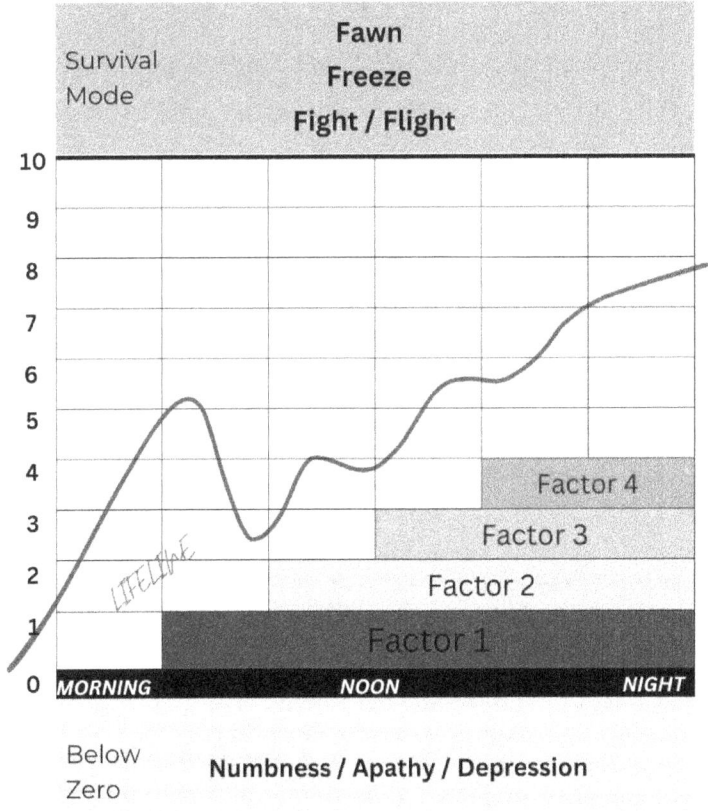

As you can see in the illustration, the top and bottom of the 'window', represent the limitations to which a person can cope. Someone can be placed at whatever height within the window, according to how a person is feeling at that moment. This placement is usually relative to a number of, what I will refer to in this book, as 'factors' pertaining to them at that moment.

Looking at the Window

Factors can be historic, recent, or present-day. They may even be generational, environmental, or societal. They are whatever forces are contributing to the emotional/mental state of that individual. On the diagram, they present much like 'stairs' each is a 'step' stacked on the other, leading upwards, elevating someone through their 'Window of Tolerance', affecting how they feel and how much 'coping' they have in reserve (above them). Until they eventually reach their limit. When a person reaches their ceiling or edge; their tolerance ceases, and their 'survival mode' kicks in. Their brain completely switches gear into a different state of being, what we call Fight or Flight, or more accurately Fight/Flight/Freeze/Fawn.

It may only be a small thing that pushes them over the edge to where they are no longer coping. We often hear sayings like "The straw that broke the camel's back" and "I had my last straw", that example how it was only a small thing that finally pushed that person to where they could no longer tolerate whatever was going on. Although, there may have been a series of things that led up to that point. People will also express where they are on the Window of Tolerance with sayings like "It pushed me over the edge", "I'm at the end of my rope", "there's not enough room on my plate", "I can't give from an empty cup" or "They've hit rock bottom".

Looking at the Window

It can be helpful to use the window to 'connect the dots' of where you have been over a series of time. This looks more like a timeline, a horizontal line that often resembles waves, rising and falling as it goes along. I refer to this line as your lifeline. In many ways it will resemble the image on a heart monitor, but with more variation.

This allows us to get a concept of the patterns and trends of your functioning and how it may have been affected over a period of time. There may be sharp precipices that seem to come out of nowhere, indicating a sudden panic with immediate reassurance (like if someone gives you a fright and then the sense of safety is quickly restored). Or there may be a pattern of large rolling waves that reach far to the edges over the months. (People experiencing hormonal factors will often express this is a pattern they can relate to.) If these waves or spikes are occurring more rapidly, within the day, you may be looking at daily factors, i.e. are you getting a blood sugar level drop at 3 because you are too busy to eat lunch?

It is quite normal for different developmental stages of our lives to have more dramatic movements through the Window of Tolerance (*cough* Toddlers, Teenagers cough**). A baby and toddler's brain has not developed to the capacity in which they can tolerate much emotional or mental stimulation at all, and hence they can quite easily elevate into the upper levels of the window. Any transitional stage of life (Puberty, Mid-Life Crisis, Divorce, Grief, New Parenthood) will create additional factors for the individual to contend with, elevating them to a naturally higher place on the window, meaning their 'room to move' is tighter before they are in a stressed, reactionary or survival state.

What is also an important observation, is how long someone spends at any level of the window. Some ebbs and flows are completely healthy, but just as an erratic lifeline jumping up and down all over the place isn't great, if someone's line isn't moving up or down much at all, this could either indicate they have always been totally content or that they have an underwhelming amount of excitement in their life. However, just as likely something more concerning could be going on.

Living for too long with a lifeline out of the window, in survival mode is exhausting. Not just to the person and their whole body, but often to people around them. Living permanently above the window can be a sign of unresolved grief, trauma, or low resiliency. There is sometimes a possibility their presentation could be connected to PTSD (Post Traumatic Stress Disorder), an anxiety disorder, or something else. Living here, without much respite into the lower/middle window, to catch their breath; being full-time in that heightened state of hyperarousal is like overworking a muscle. There is only so long it can hold on to the overbearing weight without dropping it. What happens when that happens? When the nervous system says enough?

It shuts down to protect itself. The 'muscle' drops the weight to protect itself from tearing. And this is when a person's position on the window drops from that great height to below the window; 'below-zero'. Where they will 'flatline' there, not feeling anything, not caring anymore about anything, numb, depressive, and apathetic. Until they re-emerge.

A re-emergence will usually follow a similar trajectory of going back to above the window before de-escalating down the Window of Tolerance from there. Sometimes they might crawl their way up from the bottom and slowly increase in stimulation and functioning, much like someone waking up in the morning from a deep slumber. Use the visual and relate to the 'window' however best suits you.

Not everyone will experience this place below-zero, nor would everyone want to. It is often a place that is associated with severe emotional pain or grief, depression, and debility. It can sometimes present with severe maladaptive coping mechanisms like addiction, self-harming behaviors, and suicidal ideation (although these things can exist in other areas on the window too). In saying that, many people who are familiar with this place may never experience these things at all. It is important to remember that this is a guide to help simplify and understand things that aren't always simple and easy to understand. To be able to write about human well-being at all, and provide categorical-type answers, we have to remember that humans and their well-being is never completely categorical. The information here must be taken in this context and where necessary, further information sought elsewhere.

With all of the above being said, wherever you are on your Window of Tolerance, however you got there, however long you have been there, whatever diagnoses you have been given or identify with, it is my belief, with the right self-awareness and care, that you can work your way towards a life where you can live happily and safely, rolling around, WITHIN your Window of Tolerance.

Looking at the Window

Figure 2. Introducing Resiliency Factors

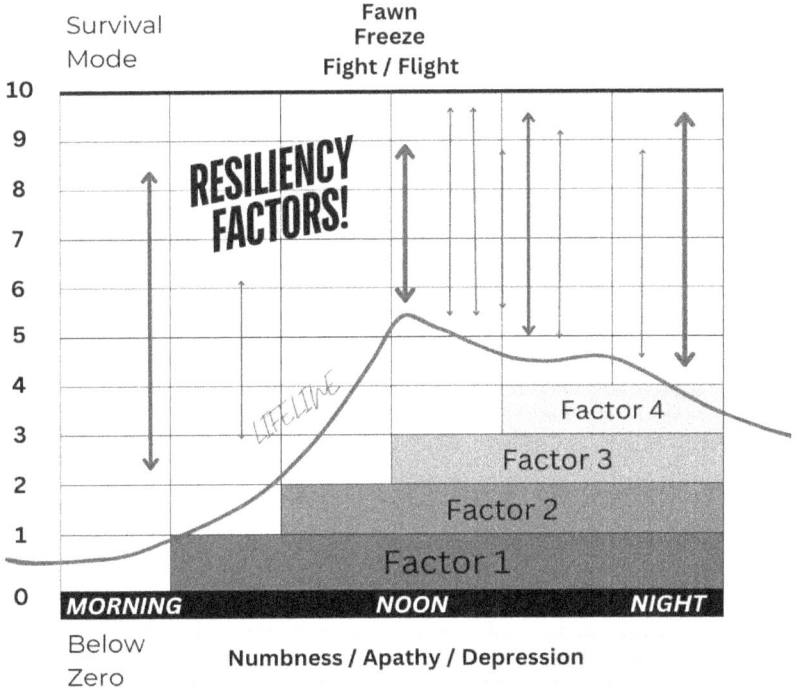

Resiliency factors are the things that help to open up this 'Window of Tolerance and make it bigger. They create a space above your lifeline and allow more room within your window. You could almost see them as an 'expanding' force that mitigates the rising levels induced by stress factors. Things that help drop your lifeline a little lower and raise the roof a little higher.

Some people are just born more resilient than others or have become that way over the course of their lives, so they have big, robust Windows of Tolerance with lots of room to move. Others may have a low level of emotional resilience in general, meaning that their 'window' might be smaller and more fragile. Either way, 'resiliency factors' are forces that any of us can introduce to our lives, to mitigate, cancel out, or allow room for the stress factors that are pushing us to the edge of our window.

All of these concepts will be explored further in the following chapters, but for now, it is good for you to internally create a good visualization of the Window of Tolerance, in whatever form and analogy that best connects with you.

The Power of Analogy

Using analogy and metaphor is a powerful, user-friendly way for people to personalize and adopt self-therapy techniques.

Some people might like to imagine the Window of Tolerance with an ocean analogy. Using this, someone's 'level' (lifeline) moving up and down through the window can be seen as waves in the ocean. I.e. "go with the flow", "rolling with the waves" etc. Increasing stress factors can be symbolized by the tide line or waves getting higher. As they grow past a level

6 a person may become more and more alert and fearful of drowning. What is comfortable and fun, wading in the waters at one point, can become someone struggling to swim, as the tide rises to the top of the 'window'. The person may 'tread water' for a while but grows fatigued, and is soon unable to cope. Alternatively, they may feel the waves have grown too big and powerful and soon enter Fight / Flight. You will hear sayings like "I'm just keeping my head above water", "I'm drowning over here" or "I'm in over my head".

Ironically, the physiological symptoms of someone going through this process on land due to stressors, is similar to that of someone in the water, fighting for their life. These include increased heart rate, gasping for breath, hyperventilation, panic, looking for safety or an exit, and rapid movement of limbs.

Figure 3. Ocean Analogy

As you can see in Figure 3, this person has escalated up their window in a series of waves. After being in Fight or Flight for some time, their lifeline then plummets to below zero (as discussed earlier). If you're familiar with how extremely large waves suck up the water from in front of them to give them extra power, you will see the analogy continues to perform with accuracy. The wave 'exhausts' the water stores in front of it, in its efforts for more capacity. Just as we do in survival mode.

Don't you just love nature for its symbolism? There is so much similarity to humans, right down to their intricate workings. It's a great reminder of how of the earth we really are.

Volcanoes are a good analogy and visual to use. Especially relatable for people who display aggression as their Fight / Flight response and are trying to work on emotional regulation to control their anger. The Volcano is at eruption when it gets past 10 and 'the lava bursts out and burns people nearby' for example. Kids especially seem to like this metaphor. A chart/picture can be used for a child to visually demonstrate where they are on their 'Volcano'. Giving these kids a way to communicate effectively, something they may not be able to achieve verbally, especially if they're above a level 6 and feeling 'worked up'.

Some people like to imagine their Window of Tolerance more as a brick wall that is slowly being built by 'factors' and enclosing them. It can feel like they are 'blocking' out the light as they increase in number. Is your tendency to 'block people out' when you become stressed? Do you feel better able to connect with people when your stress levels are lower? Resilience factors can be seen as knocking some bricks down or making a bigger window, thus allowing more light in and allowing more connection.

Looking at the Window

I had one guy say he imagined an electrical multi-box that had too many plugs in it. It was like it was drawing too much power and would start sparking and overloading until it caught on fire (Above a 10, survival mode). I thought this was a great analogy because those things often have a safety fuse button that 'pops' to protect the circuit, which is similar to what I was talking about when our nervous system shuts down to protect itself. This also gave great symbolism to work on what could be done to address this overload. Are there some plugs that could be pulled out, even just for now? Could they take turns being plugged in? What other things could we do to increase the capacity of this multi-box and power outlet to cope? Does the power source need improving? Does the grounding need improving? He was able to talk about all this in an electrical sense (that I had little idea about), and then we were able to translate these solutions back to things he could do in his real life, to have a similar effect.

If at any point you thought, 'Just find another wall socket and plug some shit in there' then you are indeed a genius, or at least a nice pragmatic thinker with some basic electrical knowledge. Makes sense doesn't it? Just share the load and use a different socket. Can we compartmentalize some things to a different socket? Or better yet, sockets? Well, well, well, more on that later.

Looking at the Window

Analogies are such fantastic therapy tools! What's a visual that works for you? Run with it.

Preparation for Activities:
There are several activities throughout this book to guide you in your self-development journey. Feel free to use these as a journaling opportunity. I highly recommend having a pen and paper or a journal, available throughout this book in general. You can jot things down as you go, list relevant page numbers of significant content you want to revisit, and use it to 'freestyle' whatever thoughts, feelings, or reflections you have while reading. Having things written down is helpful for later reflection on how far you've come but also helps to get what's on the inside, out in the tangible world, for a more objective processing of it.

Although, that said, if it suits you better, you can also just do them in your head. Don't let logistics be a barrier.

Activity. 1 - Draw Your Own Window

- Our first activity is pretty self-explanatory. Draw up your own Window of Tolerance, using the first image (Figure 1.) as a guide. You can make it as long as you like, for the last week, month, or the last few years. Pinpoint your

highs and lows and then connect the dots, or just freehand what your lifeline felt like over this time.
- You can also take a 'zoomed out' snapshot of your whole life. Draw a long window, and roughly divide it up over your lifespan. Mark your 'level' at various significant events or ages, and then link them all together to show your lifeline. Or again, you can be more expressive and freehand how this lifeline felt through the ages.
- You don't have to be too tidy or careful with these drawings, no ones marking them. They're just for you. The gold is in the process, not the finished product.

I recommend doing this activity again at the end of this book and using it going forward, as a reflective, self-therapy technique.

4. Looking Through the Window: Life Examples

The Ideal

To get more familiar with the window and how it applies to our lives, let's first take a look at how it applies to others. As an example, let's say a relatively basic human wakes up in the morning and they are on the ground floor of their Window of Tolerance. Level Zero, meaning they have no stressful factors implicating their ability to cope and have all this free room above them to expand into without getting anywhere near stress, let alone meltdown. (This person would have to have no previous trauma or unresolved adverse events in their life….so they probably don't exist, but for the sake of simplifying this explanation, this is where we're starting.)

They wake up, fresh as a daisy, probably in a relatively comfortable home, functioning at a relatively high level, with a relatively healthy sense of self-worth. If

Looking Through the Window : Life Examples

the day goes well, they may get home early that evening and still be close to the bottom of the window. They stay hydrated and are surrounded by prosocial supportive peers and superiors. They may have bounced along it a little, perhaps when the coffee shop girl mispronounced their name and everyone looked at them, or when there was a fire drill at work, or when they realized there was a typo in the email they had already sent, but in all, they stayed in the 1-4 ratio of the window. They happily said no to staying late after work because they are ok with setting and affirming boundaries and didn't even feel bad about it later. They went to their weekly Yoga class, then went home and had a healthy, nutritious dinner because they could afford it, with their ok job. They love themselves enough to prioritize their wellbeing and they also have no reason to binge and distract their brain from their problems. They go to bed at night with a clear conscience and peaceful mind and have a rejuvenating sleep to start the day with tomorrow. To be honest, they probably have some fantastic relationship with some equally healthy, high-functioning, self-respecting partner. Life sure is great for Simple Suzy (let's call her Suzy).

Looking Through the Window : Life Examples

Escalation / De-escalation

Now imagine, across town, Judy wakes up, she barely slept, she has a 1-year-old and a 3-year-old that still aren't sleeping through. She's already above level 2 before she opens her eyes. She looks in the mirror and immediately feels bad about herself. She has dark circles, dull skin and she hasn't had her hair done in over a year. She feels undesirable and is reminded of the feelings of disconnection between her and her partner. She is now at a level 3-4. She tunes out getting screamed at by the kids while making their breakfast and slaving to their every need (level 5). She forgets one of their sweatshirts when she drops them off at DayCare for the day. She feels guilty about it all day, worries if they will get cold, and fears they will get sick again (level 6). She gets to work late, is underperforming in her role, due to too many days off with sick kids and not having the same creative thought and passion when she is there. Her team leader makes a snide remark about it at the staff meeting (level 7). She notices a group of colleagues stop talking when she enters the lunch room and she then ruminates on it. Whether it's about her, her lack of productivity, her appearance, her newfound boringness, or something else. The social isolation of her current life pains her and now at level 9, close to the top of the Window of Tolerance, she is fighting

Looking Through the Window : Life Examples

back tears for the rest of the day. She remembers a time at high school when she was unincluded from a group of friends and started to feel like maybe she was unlikeable (level 10). She feels a headache coming on, starts to lose perception of detail in her surroundings and just feels foggy. She is having trouble focusing, is not present in the moment, and just wants to get home. She picks up the kids late again and gets reprimanded by the DayCare manager. Then she yells at the kids in the car for being noisy and makes them cry even louder.

Judy is now past level 10, outside of the Window of Tolerance and no longer 'coping'. She is entering Fight, Flight, or Freeze. She gets home, grabs a packet of chocolate chip cookies and a bag of Doritos and goes to her bedroom and cries (A Flight response, an attempt to mentally/emotionally run away or escape, whilst still being physically present). Or maybe she throws back a few glasses/bottles of wine (escapism/Flight), while making dinner and spits nasty words at her partner when they get home, initiating a yelling match (Fight response). Or maybe when Judy's partner comes home and sees her drinking, or crying, he yells at her, overwhelming her emotions even more, to the point Judy feels so cornered and unable to cope, that she shuts down and goes still (Freezes). She can

Looking Through the Window : Life Examples

no longer speak, think, feel. She is just frozen and a numbness washes over her body.

Lucky for Judy, she has some 'resiliency factors' in her life. Judy finds it hard to get to sleep but once she is, the kids let her sleep through. In the morning she calls her very supportive and loving Mother (who is a huge resiliency factor for Judy). They arrange some self-care outings for the future (Instilling hope, connection, and more resiliency). Judy's Mother gives her reassurance and affirmation (Mitigating some of her poor self-esteem) and also convinces her to take the day off from work (Time to sleep, rest, and unwind more resiliency). Already Judy is back, well within her window, when her partner gets home. Having reflected on the situation, as an imperfect yet loving partner, they apologize, express empathy and acknowledgment for what Judy is dealing with, and put things right. At least 40% of the stress factors have been mitigated for Judy within a day. Her headache is gone. Her heartache is gone. She feels at peace and hopeful. She is able to think more clearly about her situation at work and come up with some solutions. She is able to apply more patience and empathy to her parenting, getting more joy from the interactions with her children (building even more resiliency).

Looking Through the Window : Life Examples

Above, Below, and Back Again

Let's say, our third girl Lucy, has an almost identical bad day to Judy. When she enters the Freeze state that night, it is not a foreign place to her at all. She has lived in and out of this place for some time. She then, like Judy, goes to bed unable to sleep. Yet she wakes, still outside of her window, unable to function enough to find a solution or do anything to help herself. It is like Freeze but not so surface level, not temporary. It is something else.

She does not feel. She is on autopilot. Going through her day like a robot. She no longer cares about whether the kids eat their breakfast or have a warm jersey to wear. She doesn't care about her work. She doesn't care if she loses her job because she's unable to use the cognitive functioning that enables her to predict consequences, i.e. what will happen if she does. She doesn't care about herself anymore. She doesn't care about others. Lucy knows this place well. She thought she was doing alright for a bit… but here she is. Back in the familiar land of depression and apathy. A place beyond the survival mode. Where the nervous system is so shut down, it has no idea how to reboot itself. Weeks can go by where Lucy can live in this state… often months, years.

Looking Through the Window : Life Examples

In this scenario, Lucy didn't just have a bad day or year. Things have been bad for Lucy for a while. Lucy had a pretty dysfunctional childhood that she never really processed. Hearing domestic violence through the walls at night, A Father she mostly saw on his way in or out of the door, and a strained relationship with a Mother who just liked to sweep things under the rug and fake a smile, Lucy hasn't woken up a morning in her life anywhere under a 3.

She coped ok, in the 5-8 range much of her childhood, internalizing most of her pain. Until High School, when a boy who she thought was her friend, sexually assaulted her in her bedroom, when they were hanging out. She tried to pretend it never happened. Having no close nor trusting relationships with anyone else, she never spoke of it, nor processed any of it since. Instead, she just started living in a reactive, defensive place, level 8 and above and navigated life from there.

Her 'Fight or Flight' behaviors presented as disengaging from school, dropping grades, drinking, and participating in various high-risk behaviors. She experienced various other traumas in this time she was too dysregulated to even register as such. Her previous' people pleasing' as a child living in the 5-7 zone, became pushing people away and testing them at every turn. She had almost no stress tolerance and

Looking Through the Window : Life Examples

when triggered would tend to 'Flight' as quickly as possible to get out of a situation. She would just turn and leave, like what the inner child within her just wanted to do all those years ago, to find safety. Lucy eventually physically 'ran away'. She moved from town to town, job to job. When she met her now Husband, he represented a love and security she always wanted... in a familiar anxious way, that always made her have to 'work' for love and confirmation of her worth. She was easily manipulated into a life that served him and has since been living with very little resiliency factors, trapped in a trauma bond of abuse and codependency.

Having children added even more factors to 'push her over the edge'. After living consistently in survival mode for a few years, eventually 'the floor gave way beneath her' and she plummeted to 'below-zero'.

The reason we picture 'below-zero' this way is to represent the nervous system that has been struggling up high in the Fight, Flight then Freeze zone for too long. Lucy even moved into another survival mode Fawn, (which we talk about later) where she tried to appease and submit to her partner as a way to survive. With nothing else in her life 'giving way' and no respite back into the window to recuperate, she now had nothing keeping her propped up. Not enough

Looking Through the Window : Life Examples

resiliency factors in her life to mitigate insurmountable stress factors; trying to maintain an impossible level of functioning, under impossible levels of stress, she eventually just flat-lined. When she had nowhere else to run, nowhere to turn, and no perceivable ability to change her situation, her nervous system just shut off, as if to save itself from further damage. She began merely existing in her life, in this below-zero form. A thick, anesthetic fog, shielding her 'frayed nerves' from the harshness of the chaotic world she seemed somehow to re-create around her.

Because I just can't leave a story here, I am going to add that one day, whilst going through the paces of the day, robotic, without feeling, something happened to bring her back. Something happened to trigger her out of flatlining, like a surgeon using the paddles to resuscitate a patient, she was shocked back to life and started fighting for life.

Her partner started yelling insults at one of her kids. Derogatory, belittling, insults, tearing away at his small sense of worth. Intimidating him with his large statue into a frozen, trembling, little leaf. Lucy looked at this scene that usually had her at the receiving end and seeing the face of a small human that she loved more than herself, she felt... suddenly... she felt something... for the first time in a long time she felt...

Looking Through the Window : Life Examples

and the pain of this feeling, watching her little boy go through the fear and self-loathing she had known too much in her life, caused an animal-like sound to erupt from her body. She didn't just 'speak back', she roared like a fucking, mama lion. She stopped her husband in his tracks and she found her 'fight'. So long had she been hiding from conflict, violence, anger, anything that reminded her of that dark place as a child. But no more. She would not allow her children to live with the harm she had experienced, and she stood up to her husband and said no more.

From here anything could have happened, maybe she left him, maybe he changed, maybe they both worked on things, her on her assertiveness, and him on his verbal aggression and his own 'Window of Tolerance'. Whatever happened, let's just say something eventually gave and she was sparked back to life. For some, this spark may be a conversation with a friend that makes them feel seen and worthy of fighting for. It may be doing an activity that they love and that reminds them of who they truly are. It will be different for everyone, but this is where the Fight reflex is important. This is its real purpose. To save you. Not to be misused, or abused, like what Lucy's Husband was doing. Not to get power OVER others, but to have power WITHIN, to stand your ground when you need it.

Looking Through the Window : Life Examples

At some point, Lucy didn't need to be so much in 'Fight' mode. One way or another, she created a life, with loads of resiliency factors, where she was safe enough to hang out in the comfort zones of her window, where just being quietly assertive was enough. She was happy and strong and achieved the things she wanted in life.

Side note: Abuse of power

Additional moral of the story: If your physical or emotional safety is ever at risk or threatened, or that of someone you love, then full permission to use the necessary extent of your Fight or Flight response in its appropriate form. That's what it is there for. However, excessive use of this to the situation, gaining more power or control than what is yours to take…then there is probably something fucking wrong with you (wink wink, not really, but there is some work to do).

Hot tip: Ask yourself if you're reacting to a current situation as if it were a past situation, where you were ACTUALLY at risk. Many people that act like bullies; dominant, aggressive, defensive, abusive, asserting power OVER, or violent behaviors, have often been subject to situations where they were bullied and

Looking Through the Window : Life Examples

without power and never want to feel like that again. So they 'get others before they get them' and react to the full extent of the worst threat they've ever known, with the slightest challenge or feeling of being out of control. If that's you, congratulations on reading this book and taking accountability for this dickhead behavior. Even getting past the title shows you want more from yourself and life than what you've previously been creating. You don't want to be that person who loses everything because they can't possibly get over themselves enough to be vulnerable and fallible. So stop that shit. Keep reading. This is how.

5. Getting to Know Your Window

Factors

By now you'll have a pretty good idea of what I'm referring to by the term 'factors', but let's just investigate this a little more.

In this book, I label factors as the challenging influences, though I hesitate to categorize things strictly as good or bad, positive or negative. Life encompasses a spectrum of experiences, some of which, while demanding, also bring richness and fulfillment—such as raising children, writing a book, or doing both while running a company. All great things that bring life satisfaction, but factors all the same.

Some elevation in the window is not a bad thing. If Simple Suzy never escalated over a level 3 for months, she might start feeling completely underwhelmed, question her purpose, and digress into a mild depression below-zero. Factors are not something we want to get rid of altogether, it's about balance.

At times I've labeled factors as 'stress factors' to distinguish them from resiliency factors, yet they may not fit with your connotations of 'stress'. They could instead be challenging, disheartening, draining, consuming, upsetting, irritating, or even exciting, an obsession or passion. Essentially, they're the elements testing your resolve, pushing you up the window.

Activity. 2 - My Factors

Below is a list of some of the different factors to start contemplating. We have referenced a few already in the above examples, but start thinking about what ones might pertain to yourself or others you know.

Working through the following list, write down what factors are relevant to you. Elaborate on the factor if there are details that come up for you, as you are reflecting.

Current-day External Factors
We're talking about daily life...
- Work; projects, deadlines, remuneration, relationships, To-do lists, conflicts, etc.

- Lifestyle; social events or commitments, alcohol or drug use, etc
- Home; state of shelter or lack thereof, sense of safety, family, flatmates, and support systems.
- Money: spending to earning ratios etc.
- Tasks and chores
- Dependants and what's happening with them.
- What else can you think of?

Current-day Internal Factors
Things related more to you and how you think or feel daily
- Your level of self-esteem. The internal way you talk to yourself.
- The way you feel about yourself.
- The way you feel about other things in your life; your job, spouse, children, car, house, friends, life.
- Physical ailments or injury pertaining to your body.
- What else can you think of?

Previous Factors
Things either internal or external, that have happened recently or happen occasionally, that are still affecting you.
- Something someone said once that you still mull over.
- Something you said once.

Getting to Know Your Window

- The way someone looked at you.
- The thing you weren't invited to.
- That fight with your partner / boss / colleague / friend / parent two months ago
- What else?

Historical Factors
Things that have happened in your lifetime that either currently still cause pain or stress, or can when it is triggered and brought up.
- Parental divorce
- Growing up in poverty
- Physical, sexual, emotional, psychological abuse or neglect
- Lack of love and protection
- Lack of attention
- Trauma
- Loss
- Just about anything in childhood or your life, that left you with a lasting level of upset.
- You'll know what yours are, without judgment or justification, write them down and validate them and yourself.
- What else? That time the teacher said that thing….write that down too.

Generational
What have you inherited and how has this affected you?

Getting to Know Your Window

- Physically
- Aesthetically
- Mentally
- Behaviorally
- Norms and values
- Traditions
- Culturally
- Ethnically
- Generational trauma
- Generational curses
- What else? There are no wrong answers.

Sociological Factors
Whatever's going on in the wider community, country, and world around you. Just look how these Covid years have affected everybody.
- Politics
- Policies
- Trends
- Technologies
- News
- Media / Social Media
- Laws
- Social Constructs
- Religion
- Information
- Propaganda
- Weather

Getting to Know Your Window

- Fashion
- Whatever…I mean, what else?
- The most obvious perhaps being War. Imagine a whole country of people in fight or flight, some in freeze. How many people are still flatlining long after the war? How that then turns into historical and then generational factors.

I'm sure there are a million other factor categories but just keep going. Make your list. Better out than in. Even just shedding light into dark places makes the scary skeletons in there lose their power.

If you are feeling overwhelmed at all by the amount of 'digging around' and 'unearthing' that we do in this book, please take some time. Go make a cuppa, chill out, and take a breath. Refer to the 'De-escalation: First Aid' activity in this book, for some effective grounding and 're-earthing' techniques, to apply safety and comfort throughout our work.

Self-work, like any other kind of work, needs breaks and little holidays, to give our brain and body rest. You will need to stay somewhere within your window to be able to even process what I am writing about anyway, so start using these exact principles now and put them into practice. You don't have to be a Zen Monk but if you feel like you are getting too agitated, feeling 'out of it', 'off' or even feeling defensive, it could be a sign you're peaking into Fight or Flight. By all means take the time you need to process what's come up, before continuing. Your self-awareness and care, as a way of life, starts now.

"Slowly, slowly, quickly." — Someone once said this to me about the therapeutic process. For some reason, it has always made so much sense.

The Check-In

Learning to 'Check-In' with yourself is such a fundamental skill for self-therapy. By learning to 'check in,' you gain insight into your current challenges, their severity, and also your own inner wisdom to find the way through them.

In this method of Checking-In, I utilize what we have previously discussed about the 'Window of Tolerance' and integrate it with other therapies like DBT (Dialectical Behavioral Therapy), Solution Focused Therapy, and a few other Evidence-Based approaches that you probably don't need to get too caught up on at this stage. You can perform these steps as a complete sequence like a self-therapy session (recommended to do regularly for psychological 'maintenance') or can use them individually, conducting mini check-ins throughout the day.

I'm sure you will develop your own style, analogies, and visualizations, as you become more familiar with the practice. It won't always feel like a long clunky 'activity' either. You will soon be able to check in with yourself, within a matter of seconds/minutes, anywhere, anytime. As you grow accustomed to the prompts, your brain will create neuro-pathways that quickly get to work responding. The practice itself will soon be associated with relief, affirmation, and reassurance. This leads to a regulated nervous system gradually bringing you down within your Window of Tolerance.

In doing this we are already building our resilience and resiliency factors. Checking in with yourself and having awareness of your contributing stress factors, is a resiliency superpower!

I recommend taking this opportunity to get your paper or journal out again and writing things down as we go.

Activity 3 - Checking In

1. Right now, 'Check In' with yourself. Sometimes it helps to close your eyes to block

out distractions and tune in to how you feel in the moment. Imagine where you're at on the Window of Tolerance. (Visualize that image developed in Chapter 3, or you can flip back to Figure 1, for a reminder if you need)

2. **Give it a number between 0-10.** 10 being the top of the window, being overstimulated, and about to enter Fight or Flight. 0 being you are calm and completely unaffected altogether. Where are you?

3. You may be able to feel that in your body somewhere. **Where in your body do you feel it?**

4. **Describe it.** What does it feel like in there? How big is this feeling? What color is it? Shape? Do any other descriptive words come up when you think of this? What does the rest of your body feel like? What are your shoulders doing? Really get a sense of where you're at within yourself.

5. **What emotive words come up as you tune in? What are the feelings in this place?** Be brave and honest. You may be surprised by what comes up here. I just chuckled a little when I

did this. Emotions release and express themselves in all sorts of ways. If you feel emotional or like crying here, or anywhere else in this book, let it out. Even if it doesn't make sense. Emotions and crying are not the same as being 'Out of your window'. It is important we allow emotions to flow and be expressed while we are still in the window too. In fact, this can often help us to stay within it.

6. **What thoughts do you think when you tune in?** Often it is hard to access our 'thoughts' as we have so far been focusing on a feeling state (opposite sides of the brain). A way to get to the associated cognition is to ask…**What is your brain saying when you feel this?** For some reason, this helps to identify the 'thoughts' more.

7. **What is the "I am…." statement?** If the above cognition isn't already an "I am…." statement, then what would it be if they were, i.e. "I am…not good enough" or "I am…powerless" or "I am…afraid" are common statements underneath uncomfortable feelings. (However, if you are doing this exercise when you are in an ok place it might be "I am…ok" "I am…safe" "I am…connected" etc. which is where we want you to end up eventually. You don't have to feel

forced to come up with something 'wrong' with you if you actually feel great.)

The "I am…" statement is often a strong indicator of a 'core belief' or, what I call a "false truth" that you may have adopted at some point in your life. These 'false learnings' are often created by interpreting meaning from complex experiences, at ages we were too young to understand or process the events properly. A classic example is children who center the blame for their parents' divorce on themselves. Although it has nothing to do with them, children naturally process things around them as being because of them, for better or worse. So everything that happens is because "I am…not good enough" or "I am…good enough".

8. Now we're asking, **what is this about? What factors are contributing to this today / right now?** So again, within this moment, we are reflecting on your factors. What's happened today, this week, month, that is contributing to how you feel and where you are at? What may have been triggered? What relationships are contributing to this negatively? What are outside influences and what are internal influences? Are there some that your brain has

come up with that might not actually be true or real? (Our brains love to generate sneaky little paranoias and perpetuate them around our nervous system without us knowing).

There may be physical ailments that are short or long-term contributing. Think of how they are affecting your emotions and your ability to cope with life in general at this time.

Now dig a little deeper. What is contributing to your number on the scale today that is old, that is historic, that may have caused scar tissue within yourself, or even your generational line, that may have got a little triggered or 'rubbed the wrong way' today?

9. **What are your needs right now?** From this tuned-in, centered state, ask yourself what your needs are and how you might meet them. Sometimes the answer can be as simple as "You need some water", You need some sleep", "You need some quiet", or it might be a little more of a challenge, like "You need to stay firm on this and hold your ground", "You need to speak your truth", or "You need to let go, so you can welcome the new with two free hands". Take this time to listen to your inner voice and

guidance. This is a muscle that gets stronger the more you use it.

Through this process you may notice your original number start to change, it may go up or down, or up, then down. It makes sense that as we start to bravely shine light to some dark areas that we haven't before, it might change our rating within the window. If it has elevated it at all for you, please remember this is in preparation for lowering it in a real and sustainable way. Knowledge and awareness is power. Navigating a dark ocean with your eyes closed, when you have a map and directions right in front of you, is probably not going to get you where you want to go. Even the fact you have this book in your hot little hands I'd say you're brave enough to get past the confronting title and get real about sorting your shit out or understanding yourself better in the least.

If you are feeling like you need some 'grounding' after this or any other activity, please use the Desculation - First Aid, as mentioned. You can also follow this Check-In with the Light It Up Activity 7, for a positive 'round-up' of all the work done, and to close off your DIY therapy session nicely.

I also take this opportunity to remind you of the safety message at the start of this book. If any of these memories, or any of the content/activities in this book trigger you and send your rating skyrocketing to a point where you don't feel safe or you can't seem to de-escalate yourself for some time, please seek the appropriate help. None of the advice, information, insights, activities, or anything in this book is designed to replace or replicate medical or professional help where it is needed.

Accentuating the positive

'The Check In' is also a great exercise to build on and promote positive feelings, ie. happiness, love, compassion, confidence, a sense of connection, etc. If this is where it takes you, that's great. If you find yourself in a position where intentionally emphasizing and magnifying the positive would be beneficial, feel free to shift your focus in that direction. This can be particularly helpful for those seeking a lift in spirits or aiming to counterbalance excessive rumination on negative thoughts. Individuals grappling with a depressive mindset might especially benefit from a fresh perspective and highlighting the positive aspects of their lives. Just work with what comes up, we don't need to label things 'good or bad', or feel like we should only be doing 'shadow work'.

Getting to Know Your Window

If you're feeling great, with no stressors noticeable, you can find the area in your body that feels good and then follow the same steps in 'The Check In' investigating this sensation, feeling, thought, belief, etc. Learn about yourself through this 'rosier tinted' lens and find other strengths and sources of resiliency. Swim in the untapped pools of joy that are waiting for you to discover within yourself. It doesn't always have to just be the gloomy, or 'negative' stuff, to unpack. There may also be times you feel a bit self-worked or therapy-ed out. That's ok too and perhaps you need a little light and fluffy, non-reflective time for a while. The last activity in this book is of that nature. We are getting to that stuff. Trust me.

Toxic Positivity

You won't, however, find me advocating for toxic positivity, or what I call, trying to 'ice over a rotten cake'. Positivity can become toxic when it becomes a cognitive distortion or defense mechanism and is used to try to avoid the hard feelings and work we don't want to do. This can result in us gaslighting ourselves and others, compounding trauma or harm, and can happen very subconsciously too. If there are wounds that need air, if there are dark areas needing to be brought to light, then, by all means, be brave and give them the attention they need to heal and dissipate.

Getting to Know Your Window

Especially when these areas are just under the surface at this time and causing pressure within your window.

Tune into yourself and what you need on any day. Some days it is to get real with yourself, dig deep, and do the work. Other days it will be to just get through the day as best as you can, knowing there is something just under the surface that needs work or addressing later on. Just don't put it off forever. It won't just go away. Of course, if it is something you feel will need a professional to guide you through, then this is absolutely what you should do. Honor your voice and your self-knowledge. YOU are your own expert. (Just don't mistake your voice for toxic positivity and denial).

6. Functioning and the BIG Factors

We are now starting to delve more into the meaty 'cause and effect' of window extremities — The reason we can't all just sit in some lah-deedah little land, wading comfortably in the lapping tide of perfect emotional stimulation…all…the…time. As nice as that might sound.

Exploring these topics is not always going to be easy reading, because these aren't easy topics. It may be the first time you are learning about these concepts so getting your head around them all at once may feel overwhelming. For some of you more versed in self-development or human functioning, it may be basic. Either way, stick with it. Take your time. If you don't understand something just fake it, till you make it. Glaze over it and carry on. Blame it on my writing. It's my first time writing this too.

Like a good mother bird, I'm trying my best to soften the meaty bits to make it more digestible for the fledglings... but ya know. We either cover relevant stuff or we don't. It may be interesting to you or it might be an utter ball-ache. See how you go.

Brain and Body Functioning

As we near the edge of our Window of Tolerance, our brain functioning changes dramatically. If you are outside of your window, in Fight/Flight, and find it challenging to think clearly or get your thoughts together, that's completely understandable. Above the 'window,' cognitive function shifts away from rational and intellectual areas of the brain, making it difficult to concentrate or perform even simple tasks. Instead, it centers activity in the primitive brain regions focused on survival instincts.

This part of the brain isn't designed for complex analytical thinking; its primary function is to scan the environment for threats and react to them. It's geared to help you survive immediate dangers, like being attacked by a sabertooth tiger and other risks relative to a 'cave-people era' (hence the term 'primitive'). It floods your system with adrenaline helping you to react quickly on 'instinct' and directs blood to your muscles enabling you to either fight him or run from him. While this mechanism evolved for natural threats, it was probably not intended to be activated when we receive a phone call from our boss after-hours, or when our spouse asks why we are running late... yet here we are.

If someone is elevated to this level, they will need to de-escalate, to be able to cognitively function rationally. You may remember a time when you tried communicating with someone who was extremely escalated. Try to remember what their body language was like and what cues indicated that they were escalated. They may have been standing taller, have tense muscles, or maybe they had gone rigid and frozen. They probably struggled to even hear what you were saying, let alone process it and respond. My guess is they just reacted to everything you said as if it was a threat. How did this make you feel and affect you in your window?

In this elevated place, the endocrine system operates at full capacity, releasing cortisol (stress hormone), adrenaline, and other chemicals into the bloodstream. It can actually be a favorite part of the window for some people. They may even thrive here and intentionally cultivate a high-stress, action-packed lifestyle to sustain this sense of 'being on the edge'. Examples include 'Workaholics', individuals who engage in self-sabotaging, high-risk or criminal activities as a way of life, substance users, and 'adrenaline junkies' who revel in extreme sports. This inclination toward living on the edge might stem from escapism, issues related to power and control, or simply a preference for being highly productive individuals who thrive on getting shit done.

Whatever the reason for living at a highly escalated level, unpacking this before an event in your life forces you to, is a good idea. There is only so long a physiological system can function at this extreme before ailments may start to force self-reflection. Symptoms associated with adrenal fatigue, high blood pressure, muscular pain, tension, compromised immune system, headaches, or migraine begin to manifest as the body struggles to 'keep up'. We will talk more about survival mode later. For now, it's enough to just consider brain and body function and its implications at different areas of the window.

Keep in mind that it may not be your body that is the first to give out. It could be a relationship, a job, an accident, or another naturally occurring consequence that drives this lesson home. The message being, it's not sustainable without things turning to shit, one way or another.

Drugs and Substances

Substances (Alcohol, drugs, medicines, etc) can stimulate the excretion of all sorts of hormones and chemicals in the body and create a 'pseudo' (fake) sensation of being at a certain level on the window. People can get addicted to the sensation of being at that level and then keep trying to maintain that place….enter dependency or addiction. There is probably a drug to induce being almost anywhere on the window. Narcotics, for example, induce a 'below-zero' functioning. Amphetamines create an extreme, physiological peaking in the window. Prescription drugs are often designed to help a person chemically get back in the window.

Using drugs as a solution may appear to give temporary relief, however, unless medically prescribed as such, it is rarely a sustainable approach. Even then is best used in conjunction with other supportive lifestyle changes. Natural or herbal remedies can impact one's position within the window too, and not always as desired.

It's important to recognize that no 'high' is for free. There is always an exchange and a counterbalance when it comes to the workings of the window. The 'come down' is exactly that, often like a tonne of

Functioning and the BIG Factors

bricks. Alternatively, narcotic users can go from a painless fog Below-Zero to feeling EVERYTHING, including a heightened sensitivity to pain and anguish, well above the window. It's not a nice Shitstorm of extremes to live through. 'Chasing the high' is often just trying to avoid the dam awful low you set yourself up for from last time. This can be said of almost anything that creates dramatic shifts within the window. If you are concerned about your use or the effect of any substance you're taking, please discuss this with your healthcare provider.

Down the very bottom of the window, near level 1, people's brains can tend to be less active in general. Not necessarily bad for the first thing in the morning, yet with modern life demands you can see why we wake up and have coffee to kick start our brains. However, if you're already waking up at a level 3-5 or above, or are prone to anxiety, you might find coffee becoming less helpful and more of a hindrance. People sensitive to caffeine may find it elevates them right up the window straight away. That's not to say this person is overall in their life not coping and is in a total survival state. It is just their body having a physiological response like they are high on the window, while their mind will probably only be frustrated by this at a level 4. We will talk more about compartmentalizing factors into different windows later, but for now, you can see how different parts of us may be affected differently at different times.

With this dynamic in consideration, we can see how the mind and body influence each other. If you are physically outside of your 'window' due to caffeine, drugs, or any other reason causing increased cortisol excretion, your brain might begin to conjure reasons to justify your physical sensations. Even when they are not in fact contributing factors. It can start throwing ideas at you about what to worry about and perceive threats that aren't there, (fueled by overstimulation of the hyper-aware and reactionary part of your brain). This is often where paranoia and some anxieties come from.

In worst-case situations, it can create a looping of thoughts, emotions, and behaviors, that in turn perpetuate a cycle of further escalation and habituation. 'Spiraling out of control'. We can see this cycle in drug and substance abuse, but also when there are psychological 'triggers' of the physical response, like anxiety, PTSD (Post Traumatic Stress Disorder), other mental health disorders, as well as in more common presentations like trust issues or anger management difficulties.

These tricky loops can play on like stuck records while the brain works to make sense of its external experience. "They must be doing something to hurt me because I feel hurt," it says, without even a crumb of self-awareness, let alone knowledge of the root cause. If instead it said "Wow I am so jacked up (anxious / angry / under the influence) right now, I can't really trust my thoughts at this moment. I better chill out a bit before taking action", you would get an interruption of the behavioral loop and eventually a completely different life path. This illustrates again why SELF-AWARENESS is so important. It is very hard to continue acting like a fuckwit when you know your triggers and then own the responsibility of healing the root cause.

Trauma, Grief and ACEs

In lue of everything mentioned, it is easy to see how trauma and the Window of Tolerance are so connected. Almost all traumas involve an elevation out of the window, but not all elevations out of the window have a traumatic effect. I would go so far to say ALL of us have experienced something that has had a traumatic effect on us, in our lifetime. Hence, why this topic is imperative to cover, in relation to 'what the fuck is wrong with us'.

Functioning and the BIG Factors

Also…

… this is my jam. I specialize in trauma. In my view, undoing the effects of trauma (micro or massive) is basically the key to life. We don't need to be anything other than what we are and who we are… before trauma lied to us. That is healing. And it's pretty much all you need, to be magical. As magical as my little baby daughter with her cute, chubby cheeks when I look at her. To me, she is a miraculous, perfect being. Even my son who … ok this one time I hurt my own throat I yelled FUCK so loud. You don't even want to know... it was… everywhere…but he is perfect. I would walk through fire for him. You are that valuable, deserving, and magical. You may have forgotten along the way. Probably with some shitty experiences, forming shitty false learning, compounding shitty beliefs, then creating some shitty behavior. But you are still as perfect as anyone on this planet; perfectly you, at any point on your lifeline.

Unlearn the wrong learnings.

ACEs (Adverse Childhood Experiences) are a list of childhood conditions that have been found to adversely affect people later in life. Even contributing to the increase of health issues ranging from mild to deadly. These factors include emotional neglect, moving a lot, discrimination, separation from a parent, unloving or

Functioning and the BIG Factors

complicated relationships with a parent, poverty, physical/sexual violence and abuse, witnessing domestic violence, and more. Although there may be argument, as to whether all of these are considered traumas or not, rather than get too far into a debate on a complex topic, let's just accept that what we are talking about here are things that have 'had the effect of trauma' on the individual. That is something that has had a lasting adverse effect on them. What is traumatizing to one person, may not be to the other, or differing degrees and affect. What can be a trauma to one person, may even promote resiliency in another. A transition, I believe, we are all capable of with the right work, healing, path, or inclination.

Grief too has a similar effect of trauma on an individual. The loss of a loved one can be one of the biggest traumas we will ever experience in life. Just because it is a normalized trauma, that comes to most of us at some point, doesn't mean its effect is any less devastating. Finding your way back into your window, after a loss can take a lot of time and requires grace, patience, and gentleness. The same as if you had suffered a severe physical injury or any other painful event.

A trauma doesn't need to be current or recent to affect our window. Events, conditions, or circumstances at any stage of life, can be a huge factor to our current

Functioning and the BIG Factors

functioning, especially if unresolved. They can still, years later, cause an elevated state within our nervous system, sometimes without us even knowing it. It may appear they are dormant or not a factor at all, until one day they are triggered to the surface...then out through the top of the window we go, to the surprise of ourselves and probably people around us. Sometimes they can take a bit longer to emerge to the surface, like a rumbling volcano that's ready to clear off some old, built-up hot air. These times, although often uncomfortable, confusing, and a bit scary, are fantastic opportunities to get the work done, and remove or reduce these underlying, pressure-causing factors in your life. So dig deep and let them go. Letting off steam when you need to in a controlled cathartic way, is much better than a full-scale, volcanic eruption at some point because you didn't.

Traumatic experiences during childhood often remain unresolved until later in life, because a child's brain isn't equipped to process such complex events. Healing becomes even less likely while they remain in the same unsafe or triggering environment where the initial harm occurred. These unresolved issues can manifest as problematic behaviors, intense emotions, and social difficulties, often without clear connections to their underlying causes. Basically, they live above the window. Traumatized children often get diagnosed with ADHD because they can present almost exactly the same way.

Sometimes, these effects may only surface in the teenage years when the brain has matured enough to recognize the presence of trauma. It is incredible how the human mind waits for someone to be psychologically ready and capable enough before it 'sends up' the trauma to be processed. Hence why often we see a lot of things 'surface' over the teen years when there is a boost in brain development. From the outside, it often looks like they're 'going off the rails' when in reality they are just trying their best to grapple with so many new things, plus old things they've never been able to perceive with so much complexity or detail before. It can be such an overwhelming time, processing it all.

Until the trauma is addressed or even partially resolved, its emotional impact continues to reside within the individual's nervous system, perpetuating messages "I am...not safe", "I am...not lovable", "I am....not good enough", "The world is not a safe place", "The world is not loveable", "The world is not good enough". Then due to 'Confirmation Bias', looking through the lenses of these 'false beliefs', they will start to see only the things in their life and the world around them that 'confirm' and compound them, rapidly solidifying them into their core beliefs.

Functioning and the BIG Factors

This process of forming beliefs and eventually our 'world view', can happen from any experience at any stage of our life, but is most common during childhood when our brains are growing and forming these core beliefs so quickly, in order to hang other ideas and information off. I won't get too into the neuroscience but let's just say, the brain is like Play-Doh or Lego. Just because it's been a certain way for a long time, doesn't mean you can't change it. You can!! It might be a bit harder work the longer a construct has been that way, but the brain is nothing short of miraculous in its ability to change, grow, and adapt. MIRACULOUS!!!

In adulthood, we often reach a breaking point, where we have grown exhausted with these repetitive cognitive loops and how they show up in our lives. Self-sabotaging patterns, shitty relationships, people pleasing, financial struggle, and all the other things these 'False beliefs' manifest as. When we finally say "Enough! There is a common denominator here, and it's me!", or alternatively "What the fuck is wrong with me and what do I do about it?", and get to work on ourselves.

We then start the journey through the 'layers' of our trauma and the shitty things that have happened to us and around us; programming us with utter bullshit about our worth and 'false truths' about how the world is. We get riding that wave, from wherever outside of the window we have likely been living, to back within it... at least most of the time.

No matter what you have been through, each fraction of your lifeline is unique and valid. As we get better at riding the ebbs and flows of life, we can look back with more grace and strength at the waves we've overcome in the past. Viewing them in a whole new light. Including them into our life story in a completely different way. Even if now it seems insurmountable, as you build confidence in your own capacity to manage hardships, you will more easily look back at traumatic events and be able to apply the same resiliency to that time. Almost as if traveling through time and sharing your healing and growth with that younger version of you.

Big Factors Need Big Solutions

By opening up and 'cracking the door of the closet' to some of these bigger, potentially more deeply rooted, and longstanding factors, we are allowing some light into these dark places. With acknowledgment, even with a gentle nod in their direction, we are taking some power back. We are owning these situations, so that we may then do something about them. Whether Abuse, Trauma, ACEs, Addiction, Dependency, Mental Illness, or potentially a combination of them all, these 'Big Factors' typically must be addressed in some way, before you can sustain a more healthy, ebbing 'lifeline' within the window. For someone to say they are fine and they 'can handle it', whilst still doing the drugs, alcohol, or other harmful behavior that is part of the loop that puts them out of their window, then they are just lying to themselves; in denial and only prolonging their healing, peace and their own good. Only you will know what the balance, or pattern, is for you and only you can do something about it.

A comprehensive exploration of these kinds of factors is a bigger journey than what we can cover solely in this book. Hopefully, it ignites that path and gives some tools to travel it, however, you may need more to address these topics, in their own complexity also. The diversity that is trauma, mental health, or substance use/misuse, and the individual uniqueness that is yours and how you manage it, I would suggest needs focused attention and work upon, in whatever way best suits you.

Nothing about humans is an exact science and as mentioned earlier, this framework definitely is not. It is merely a fantastic tool to use however best suits you, in which to understand yourself and others better. I do not seek to explain in depth drugs, addiction, different diagnoses or cover all corners of mental health. That is a whole library's worth, maybe several. This book merely presents a simple visual concept, and explores this metaphor in relation to human emotion, functioning, and behavior, in a relatable, palatable way, to your DIY therapeutic benefit at home. With that said, we can continue to build on this metaphor, to better demonstrate and understand the complexity that is human functioning.

7. House of Many Windows

If we imagine now that your house has more than just one window. It has several. Thank goodness because how dark would a house be with just one?

We might approach life by looking out one window at a time, or we might have a primary window, front, and center, that shapes our daily functioning and perspective. However, relying on just one window isn't always sufficient. Different aspects of our lives and experiences may require us to view them through various windows to gain a comprehensive understanding and navigate effectively.

As mentioned, we may have someone presenting with an elevated, overly caffeinated state, with heightened heart rate and cortisol levels, over in their 'Physical window', but their mental state over at their 'State of mind' window might still be quite low. They've accepted that they shouldn't have had that second cup and now they are just tired and wired at the same time. Similarly, an athlete could be physically fatigued or injured but they use their mental capacity and strength to finish the race. Their Physical Window is maxed out but they use the reserves of their Mental Window to push them over the line. Provided these people don't continue having excess caffeine every day or are running marathons every second day, they may be able to keep these 'Physical Windows' from affecting their 'Mental Window', or the other windows (areas of their life) too significantly.

If we can compartmentalize our windows, this can help provide further understanding to ourselves, and also provide more empowerment over our lives and solution-finding. Have you noticed that you might have a specific window that is elevated, or highly active in its ups and downs, whereas other windows maintain a relatively grounded stable flow?

Your Relationship Window could be going through a rough patch or turned into a total rollercoaster, but your Friendships Window might be stepping up with some good resiliency and support. Then you can borrow all these 'resiliency factors' from your Friendship Window to cope with the Relationship stress. Or vice versa. It could be Work, Children, Extended Family, or unresolved trauma, coming up, and these other windows make it easier to cope with the one that is elevated for a time.

Why do we gather around our friends or family who have just lost someone? We say things like "If there's anything I can do?", and usually there isn't, but the demonstration of support alone, seems to give people emotional resiliency to get through their hard time. It really does make a difference.

If you're trying to work with just one window, your entire state of being is at a whim to whatever area of your life is the worst rating at the time. Let's imagine you're dealing with a lot of stress at work, ranking at an 8 on your scale of intensity. Then, you come home to find chaos. The kids have made a mess, dinner's late, and you start feeling like nobody respects or appreciates you. "It's like that other time this happened"…and your brain subconsciously makes links to the other things that 'confirm' this same false belief….. "I am not valued", "I am not worthy", and suddenly, your inner child is triggered…now you're out of the window, reacting like an upset 8-year-old.

Now imagine, the next day, the thing at work is resolved. You get loads of acknowledgment and praise, suddenly all is well in the world. You're excited to get home to the family and you pick up your partner's favorite food, to give them a night off cooking. However, when you get home, no one is happy to see you, because you were such a dick the night before. Now you're feeling triggered again and it's like you can't catch a break. "Why do you even bother?". Spiral. Spiral. Although we love it when the 'wins' spill over into other areas of your life, you can also see how working with one window only, our whole life is at a whim of what is doing the worst at the time. Being able to compartmentalize things at the start could have avoided the spiraling of tension and frustration. Leaving work at work, so to speak, and coming home with the same love and appreciation for the family, could have resulted in protecting the Family Window from cross-contamination with the Work stress, and also on receiving their love and support, the Work Window could also have benefitted. Setting in motion a pattern of bi-directional benefit to both areas of your life, rather than the opposite.

Now let's consider this scenario. You're walking home from the bar, and you see your ex with someone new, driving down the street. This elevates your window right up to the point where you want to run and hide down a side alley, but instead, you freeze, keep your head down, and internalize feelings of anger and regret. For the next week, you are snappy at flatmates, sleeping more, calling in sick to work, and not wanting to leave the house. Working from one window we are unable to see anything else going on in our life, other than the pain, rejection, and frustration of this one event and the attached meanings we hold to it. If we see this as its own window, say 'The recent Ex we are still not completely over' Window, then we can allow ourselves to feel hurt, sad, and vulnerable about that, even the whole relationship it brought up and all the events in it. Yet we can go home to our flat and still know we have good friends and a good life outside of that. We may even share this incident with our flatmates to get support and de-escalate that window more. We can center ourselves within a house with many windows, not just center ourselves within the one doing the worst at the time.

As a real-life example, I recently had some old unresolved 'stuff' surface, which to start with felt very overwhelming in general. I initially just had one window and it was maxed out. This was affecting all sorts of other areas of my life, my relationship, my sleep, my enthusiasm, and my self-worth. The ripple effect from a trigger of old traumas that haven't been addressed, resolved, or de-escalated down their window, can be huge. I was right back to feeling like an abandoned little girl again with nowhere to turn (that feeling of Flight response, but with nowhere to run or hide, is such a horrible vibe. If you know, you know). Once I 'Checked In', realized the exact things that were bothering me, the core memory and meaning (False Belief) that this was attached to, I was able to attribute it to its own window. Then, although this issue was still 'there' and still very much escalated, I was able to enjoy the other areas of my life. I could still receive the stability, love, and assurance I needed, while I unpacked and dealt with this other area over time. I felt a lot stronger and more supported, drawing from the resources of other secure areas, to work through the issues within this other window and implement the solutions needed. All the while knowing clearly that it was just a defined area of my life and not my WHOLE life.

If we remember back to brain function, we have so much more ability to resolve, communicate, and rationalize if we are coming from a place where our window rating is lower/mid levels, than coming from a window that is maxed out into Fight / Flight/ Freeze. We can utilize the strengths and capacity of other windows to support and advocate for our compromised or strained window. This is where compartmentalizing our windows can lead to real empowerment and better management of our lives.

I do want to add, what might appear as an obvious disclaimer; this is not the same as developing different personalities or identities. Those are very different things entirely. We also do not want to use this approach to then 'cut out' a part of who we are and forget about it to only live in the 'happier' windows, (refer back to Toxic Positivity). We utilize this more flexible notion of having a house with many windows, in which to be able to draw on all areas of our lives for strength, and resources and ultimately build our resiliency. Not to utilize it as a form of denial, avoidance, or self-neglect/abandonment.

Using the analogy of having different windows in our house, we can also acknowledge the link between them too and that they can never completely function in isolation for too long. They are still part of the same house and being. It is important to not assume that with the right 'boundaries' to each we can max them all out at once. We need some areas of ease, rest, support and security for 'life balance', while other areas may be more active or elevated for a time. If there is not an orchestrating of balance and corresponding movement around different windows, then there will be an overall burnout (exceeding level 10 then dropping Below-Zero). Where there is an extremity of elevation in one window, there is another that has to accommodate for that. You either do it with intentional management and decision making, or it happens as a naturally occurring life consequence, but guaranteed, if you're in a place where you feel like 'somethings gotta give' but you don't make any changes, the time will come when something gives.

Activity. 4 - Your House of Windows

Let's take the time to reflect on what your different windows are. Get out the pen and paper and **draw (or list) your different windows** that you feel are relative to you at this time. They may be currently active ones or are relatively dormant at the moment. This may also align with some of the factors we explored earlier in Activity 1, but gives us a more detailed look at each, and helps us to see how they have been interacting and influencing each other.

Draw where you are at in each window (or write the rating).

You may like to **come back to this every few days or weekly, to chart how you are going in each**.

Finally, you may like to **draw a line to link between various windows that you feel are strongly connected** and influence each other. You can draw a thicker darker line or a lighter one depending on how strong or influential that connection is. It may end up looking like a spider web. That's ok. There is an element of Art Therapy we are bringing in here. Lean into the artistic expression of this exercise if you feel too. Go nuts. Nobodies watching. Do an interpretive dance. Whatever works.

8. Out of the Window

Now that we've built up a good amount of self-awareness of your Window of Tolerance and the variation of factors that could pertain to it, we are going to take a deeper look at behaviors, and more so those that occur outside of the window. I could sit here writing half a chapter on the behaviors of 'Simple Suzy' who lives at the bottom of the window having a largely underwhelming yet safe life, but we're not here for that. Let's remember the title of the book. It's not called "What the fuck is right with Suzy?".

Survival Mode

Once upon a time, we used to refer to survival mode as two responses, Fight or Flight. It was the 80s, life was simpler then. However, we have since realized that there is an additional Freeze response, and also more recently the Fawn response has come to light. We can often have a dominant response we trend towards when we enter survival mode (above 10); our 'go to' or something we fast track to. If we have had a past trauma or on a lot of occasions graduated from a Fight to Flight to Freeze, we may in the future just go straight to the Freeze, or if we have spent some time in the 'below-zero' area, we may fast track to there. Countering this 'fast-tracking' can mean strengthening other neuro pathways and letting the old ones weaken. That means making new healthier responses habitual, in replacement of old reactions.

Fight

Gorilla

A reflex to fight the threat. An example is when someone gets startled and instinctively punches or lashes out without even thinking— their body automatically goes into fight mode, ready to defend or assert itself in some way. The fight response isn't always physical aggression or violence; it can also manifest as verbal aggression, intimidation, or the use of posture or size to assert dominance. Visualize how animals behave when they are having confrontations. The baring of teeth, hissing, spitting, making fists, making themselves appear taller and bigger by puffing out their chest; all of these body cues suggest someone is in Fight mode. They may act like everything you say or do is an attack. They will start making bigger body movements and gestures, they will encroach on personal space and other boundaries. They may break things or throw things around and potentially seek to control you or the situation with threats or intimidation.

Fight response can also be less obvious in its presentation and may be exhibited as passive-aggressive behaviors like more covert manipulation, sabotage, snide remarks, insults passed off as humor, criticisms in front of friends and other acts to belittle or make someone feel less than themselves. It can be anything that seeks to put one person in a dominant position, gaining power and control over another.

Although these responses are often talked about in their negative capacity, they all have their purpose and benefits. As used in the example with Lucy, Fight is a huge motivator for change. When we can not tolerate something then Fight gives us the 'Power' to do hard things that need to be done. It gives us bravery, passion, and determination. In self-defense classes for teenage girls, we taught them to access their Fight mode and to use this for their protection and survival when necessary. Most importantly, we taught them to identify if they were in Freeze and to break out of this, so that they could Fight, or ideally Flight (run away).

Fight response for someone who has done a lot of work on themselves, can look like a firmly worded, respectful communication of boundaries. You might also question someone else's intent like "Are you ok? Are you disappointed I didn't put the trash out?" when perceiving a tone, rather than launch into a defensive attack (get them before they get you strategy). This allows the other person to talk and de-escalate if they were indeed upset or alternatively allows you to clear up any misreading of cues. To be fair, this mature communication isn't the 'traditional' Fight response, because in true Fight you would be too escalated to use your rational brain enough to stay this grounded and reasonable. This is the behavior of someone very much still in the window, yet as you start to have more awareness of where you and others are in the window, this healthy zone is more where you'll stay. Then you can protect and assert yourself adequately, without getting out of control of your behavior or disrespecting others' boundaries.

Flight

Horse

The instinct to run away; to escape danger or threat. "Itchy feet", "Cold feet" and "Feeling flighty" might refer to the way we can feel in our body when the Flight response is activated. We can become fidgety and start searching for the exits in a room, "Backing off", and putting "One foot out the door". Much like Fight, Flight isn't just physically running away. It can look like avoidance, abandonment, lack of commitment, quitting, distraction, attraction to the next best thing, starting something new before finishing the last, moving a lot, 'doing a geographic' (as my Aunty called it, when I would move all over the country, and then the globe). It can look like walking away, neglecting responsibilities, 'washing your hands of something', or detachment.

There is not necessarily an order in which any of these responses happen, however, Flight can be the thing that people resort to if they have tried to assertively communicate their boundaries and they don't feel it's working. Hence, a level of threat and unsafety is perceived, and then moving away from the threat is the next best thing to do. Just as Fight will usually be attempted if Flight efforts are thwarted/blocked.

Flight has its purpose too and like all of these reflexes is designed to keep us safe and to quickly and efficiently move out of harm's way and away from pain. It is a reflex designed for the Antelope to escape the Lion, or for someone to quickly outrun an attacker. I can only assume that it wasn't an instinct designed for parents to abandon their children at the first sign of having to face one of their own areas of development. I can also only assume it was not designed so that said abandoned Children could grow up and bounce from one relationship to the next, to leave others before they were rejected themselves… and yet here we are.

Flight's purpose within the window has its importance also. It is the instinct to know when something is not right for us and the courage to leave situations when they are not. Sometimes we do need to activate our Flight instinct and permit ourselves to get out of a situation, relationship, job, or house that is no longer working for us, and not remain victim to the methods that seek to hurt or oppress us.

A healthy Flight response is not always the big gestures and complete upheaval either. Sometimes it is the rational, controlled decision-making that changes the course of our life slightly, for our benefit. It could be the ending of a conversation that is not going anywhere good or the subtle reminder that if someone keeps crossing that boundary, then you won't meet them halfway and will withdraw your part of the effort. All this happening in a respectful way within your Window of Tolerance.

Freeze

Rabbit
Freeze is the instinct of the animal that feels powerless against its adversary to win the fight and also perceives no hope in its ability to escape it. I referred earlier to that awful sensation of wanting to run away but having nowhere to turn. This caged hopelessness, and feeling

of disempowerment, gives way to such an overwhelming panic that can cause the individual to Freeze.

The freeze response is often observed in small children raised in fearful environments or adults in relationships with repetitively abusive incidents. It can often present with a tense rigid posture, shaking/shivering, and dilated pupils. In more severe cases, it can lead to dissociation, where individuals feel disconnected from both their body and their surroundings. This dissociative state can be terrifying, serving as a psychological mechanism to protect oneself from the traumatic event by making it feel less real or severe. However, when dissociation occurs as a symptom of post-traumatic stress, it can happen suddenly, long after the event, causing significant confusion, frustration, and debilitation for the individual.

Freeze comes with extremely low functioning due to a shutting down of the individual's nervous system; the purpose of which is to protect it from the physical and psychological pain it experiences or fears it will experience. It is intended as a temporary state to prevent further provoking of the threat and minimize damage to itself. What it is not intended for, is to make 'easier repeat victims', or as a long-term coping strategy while others' harmful behavior continues unchecked.

In a less obvious way, this response can be a 'Freezing out' of certain components of ourselves or parts of our reality, i.e. living in denial about harmful or disrespectful behaviors happening to, or around us. If we are living in discriminatory environments, we may freeze out parts of ourselves that are not accepted there, as an attempt to 'adapt', remain loved, and hence 'survive'. It may be a desensitization to numb the pain of a relationship that we are not wanting to sever or a confrontation we are not ready to have. Perhaps we don't think we will 'win' if a boundary is communicated or an ultimatum is given. We may have extreme fear because we don't think we could handle the truth of the situation if it were brought to light and we allowed ourselves to be honest and transparent about it. A situation where psychologically we perceive having no safe way to go, so we just Freeze, and hope it goes away.

Freeze used intentionally, within the window, is the waiting before responding. It is the time you take to allow a situation to de-escalate so you can communicate more calmly. It is the biting of the tongue when you know what you are going to say may not be helpful. It may be keeping your head down while your raging teenager processes their emotions (for the next 3+ years).

Fawn

Fawn (A baby deer)

The submissive, the appeaser, the 'pick me'. From what we have just discussed about the covert forms of Freeze, you can see how someone can then graduate further into survival mode and become the Fawn. A lesser-known instinct, but familiar to many who have encountered long-standing abuse. Have you ever seen the videos where the baby Antelope is 'adopted' by the Lioness, just after it ate its Mother? Then decides not to eat the young and instead starts to 'care' for it. That is the survival intention of the Fawn. Fawn is the Stockholm Syndrome of the Survival modes. It is the victim who does what they're told, submits, and seeks out the approval and even 'affections' of the abuser because that is where they are safest.

In such instances, abuse may be accompanied by a perceived dependency on the abuser. This could stem from the abuser controlling essential resources such as food and shelter, or the presence of threats involving children or other individuals involved. The victim might also be under the illusion that the abuser provides something they need, such as protection or drugs. They may even believe that the abuser loves them and is the only one who ever will.

Fawn is beyond the inaction of freeze. It is an action in which survival becomes more important than escape, rights, values, personality, or anything that a person previously identified with or held important. It can be a very hard place to come back from, because of the way it strips almost everything from a person, other than their bare and basic instinct to exist.

Fawn's purpose is to be the cunning captive, who wins the trust of the captor, so they can get away at the first opportunity. But like the other survival modes, Fawn doesn't just exist in the obvious extremes. What the Fawn response is not intended for, is so that 'people pleasers' can give over and above, and do crippling amounts of work, in various areas of their life, to their detriment, just so they don't have to experience the disapproval of others. So they can 'feel safe' knowing they have earned good praises…yet here we are.

Within the window, Fawn is the diplomatic negotiator. It is the building of rapport before addressing the confrontational topic. It's the empathizer and the mediator. Fawn used in a grounded sense can help build bridges between people so that there is no further escalation up the window. However, a healthy Fawn does not drop their boundaries to achieve this.

Below Zero: Flat Lining

When you've lived outside the window for too long, this can be where people plummet too; the very bottom, below the window. The home of numbness and apathy.

People here experience indifference, a coldness, a lack of emotion, and enthusiasm for things that would otherwise excite them or take their interest. They can lose sight of meaning, purpose, belonging, and consequence. Their cognitive functioning becomes implicated giving way to memory issues and an inability to see reason or make sense of simple things. They may sleep a lot, yet not feel rested. They may lose motivation towards even the most basic daily tasks, getting dressed, showering, making the bed, personal hygiene, and their presentation. Unlike Freeze and Fawn, where there is still emotion and stimulation of the nervous system, here there is usually not.

The reason this place can be of such concern is that before where there was at least concern, fear, and a strong instinct to survive, here, this may cease altogether. Meaning someone no longer cares if they survive or not. Some may even want to stop living.

Out of the Window

To be in a place like this is extremely sad, and even to discuss and bring light to this as a subject can be upsetting to many. Especially to those who have experience with either their own or someone else's suicidal ideation or suicide. However, it wouldn't be right to leave out or ignore this extent of the scale, just to avoid this trigger. I live in a country with some of the worst suicide statistics in the developed world. There are many theories as to why this is, but there are no 'excuses', in my view, for our people, young or old, to feel that they have nowhere to turn, in a relatively knowledgeable and lucrative society. Opening up about these topics, discussing them, and shining the light into these dark places that people fear to talk about, is only going to help the people who are in those places, who are feeling alone, unseen, and in the dark. You are seen, I see you, We shine the light on your situation right here, now with these words and you are not alone. We are all with you, reading these words together. Let this light illuminate your way out. See that you have a ladder, and you can climb back up. You just have to grab it, hold on and take the first step. Find your fight.

Again, I remind you of the safety message at the start of this book. If what has just been talked about applies to you or someone you know, please reach out and get the help you need. Take that first step. Don't stop reaching out, and don't stop doing the things you need to, to get back to where you need to be. Where you are feeling like you want and deserve to be here, because you do. You are a part of the earth and sky and universe and we, the collective whole, need you. If you have been enduring this 'flat-lining' and want it to end, know that the rest of the window is there, waiting for you to experience so much more in your life. You have access to it all. This place doesn't last forever, you will make it back. Believe in you. I believe in you. I have seen many people, exactly where you are, in this dark place, who are now living happy, wonderfully fulfilled lives. Lives they couldn't ever have imagined from that dark place. Don't give up. Reach out. Hold on. The ladder is there. Leading to the light.

Suicidal ideation isn't always a part of this place 'below-zero'. For some people, it is not a concern here. It also pays to mention people can still experience it in other areas on the window. Often if they have been 'below-zero' before they can be more easily triggered back to these elements of it. However, it is important not to stereotype people at risk and assume they will present a certain way because this is very often not the case. Keep talking to your loved ones and keep them close. Don't be afraid to ask them directly if you are worried about their safety. If it is at risk, connect them with support, because you will both need it.

Anyone who is in this place 'below zero' will need support. Rally around them, and if it is you, let people in. Start climbing and get to a place where you can start making the changes you need to, live above that line. Sending light and blessings with these words for your journey. You've already begun it if you're reading this book.

No Window of Tolerance?

Figure 4. When you don't have a Window of Tolerance

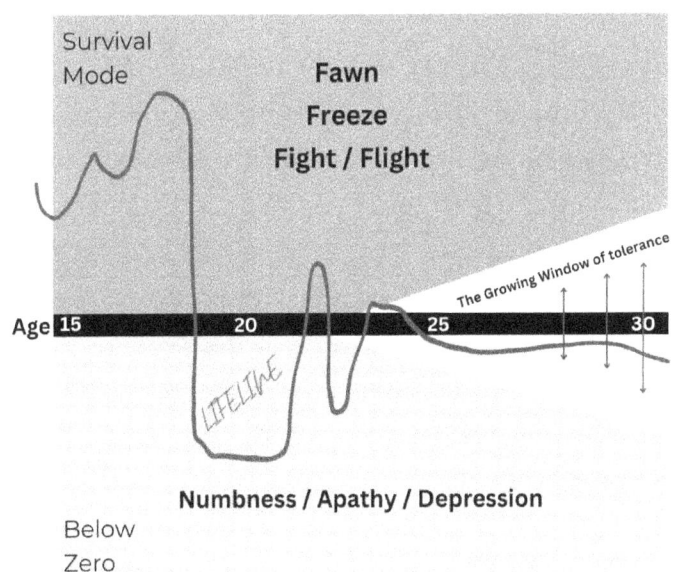

Out of the Window

This image is an example of what life might feel like if someone has almost no Window of Tolerance at all. They seem to go from above, to below, without much room in the middle. Just living their whole lives in either survival mode or below zero. Sometimes going between the two quite rapidly and unpredictably. A difficult and exhausting ride indeed. However, it is very understandable to feel this way. Particularly for a time, after a huge loss or trauma or when we are young, don't have many pre-existing resiliency factors, or have endured big, overwhelming factors. This becomes even more prevalent if we have a combination of all of these things.

If you look at the ages illustrated on the graph, it almost completely coincides with brain development. As we get older, the development of the Frontal Lobe in the brain (that only becomes substantial in its function around age 20 - 24), helps us to take more control of our lives. Over this time we get better at forming resiliency factors, processing difficult experiences or emotions, and more easily find solutions to challenges, opening up a Window of Tolerance, where there may not have been one before.

The Prefrontal Cortex in this part of the brain, is vital for predicting the consequences of our actions, so being able to 'forecast' forward, we start to navigate life with a whole new ease. Tolerating stressors with so much more capacity than before, knowing that feelings don't last forever and tomorrow may be different. Over time, with continual learning, developing, and healing, we can have a life that looks however we want it to.

This is why it is very important people do not make permanent decisions, or take risks with permanent consequences, while in extremes of the window, particularly when they are young. Although, this also explains why so many do at this stage of life.

Living life feeling like you have 'no window', is not strictly reserved for youth. The rollercoaster from top to bottom with no rest in between, can be experienced by anyone at any age. Temporarily, it is the normal aftermath of a massive loss or trauma, but a long-standing lifeline like this would indicate a number of much more complicated, and unresolved, factors. Sometimes these people are adults with children of their own. Can you imagine what it is like for a child with a parent who has almost no Window of Tolerance? (Some of us don't have to imagine too hard).

Here seems a good time to reflect on how our own windows affect the children in our care. Your children basically live in your window with you. What is below-zero for a parent, can look like isolation and neglect for the child. What is Fight / Flight for the

Parent, can be abuse or abandonment. And so on and so forth, the generational cycles continue. Let's end that shit. It stops with you.

Behaviors: What are yours?

Activity. 5 - What do I do? What can I do?

Take some time to reflect on what your behaviors are in different places throughout your window. Again, you can do this in your head, or write it out. Whatever works best for you. I will probably release an accompanying journal to do these "What the Fuck is Wrong With Me?" Activities, so keep an eye out, but for now, just use what you got.

Part One:

1. **Set up: Draw (or imagine) a large window on your page.** Leave lots of room at the top and bottom, with the 0 - 10 rating on the left-hand side, from 'ground level' / Zero up. Divide the length of the window into 3 columns, making each as spacious as you can.

2. **In the <u>First Column</u>: Write at the different levels the sort of thing you do when you

reach each place. Be honest with yourself. I start to get impatient and a bit snappy, probably about a 6 or 7. I noticed this the other day and 'Checked In' with myself to realize I hadn't eaten properly all day and my blood sugar level was lacking. Having a well-balanced snack brought me down to about a 4, so I was much better placed to get the daily tasks done, as well as deal with the other factors that were now only a minor pain in the ass.

3. **In the <u>Second Column</u>: Write things like body cues;** 'I get tension in my jaw', 'My shoulders get tense', and 'I get a headache', or whatever your ones are, at the corresponding levels. **Include also any feelings or thoughts that you might feel at each level.** Note too, if there is a lack of feeling or thinking at any level.

4. **Think** of how you behave when you are at an 8, getting closer to a 10. Do you realize when you are escalated and at the top of your window, at the time? **If you had an 'inner child', what are they doing at this level?**
What is your behavior at a 10? What is your inner child doing now? **What are you able to do at that stage to bring yourself back down?**

Ask yourself these similar questions for the lower levels of the window. What is your inner child doing/feeling when you are at these lower levels?

5. **At what level do you start to not feel comfortable? Is there anything about the higher levels that you DO like or that makes you feel good? Is there anything about the lower ones that you DON'T like or make you feel uncomfortable?** The answers to this may surprise you, as often we subconsciously avoid the lower levels and don't even know why. Sometimes lower levels are not enough stimulation for us or can remind us of a below-zero feeling and we want to run from that. Even being inside the window may deter you for some reason. It all makes sense. Write it all down. Feel free to turn a page and just write what comes up with these questions.

6. **In the <u>Third Column</u>: Do you do anything to de-escalate and calm yourself at any given level? If so, then what?**
What are some things you could start doing to de-escalate and bring your rating back down at any given level? This list is like tools in your tool belt; Resilience factors. Some things you will do already. Good on you. There

is always room for more. Add to the list and re-create this window as often as you like.

Part two:

7. **How do you Behave when you are out the Top of the window?** Are your behaviors more Fight, Flight, Freeze, or Fawn? Are they a mixture of these?

8. **What are your body cues at these levels?**

9. **What are you thinking or feeling?** Are you thinking at all? How easy is it for you to think at this level?

10. **What is your inner child doing at this level?** What do they need? What memories does this remind you of?

11. **What do you do to de-escalate at this time? What else could you do to de-escalate at this time?**

It may be helpful to try to remember the last time or other times, you were triggered to above a 10 to try to remember accurately what it is like. Sometimes it can be hard to remember details of what we are like or what is happening when we are out the top of our window because, as mentioned, our brain functioning is not overly active in rational or complex functioning areas at the time.

Part Three:

12. **Do you have any experience of being Below-Zero?**
    When was that?
    What contributed to you being there?
    When/How did you get out?
    What kept you safe or cared for you, while you were there?
    Do you see any purpose to your time there, i.e. rest, recuperation, protection of the nervous system?
    Did you learn anything from this time?
    Do you need to go back and give this version of yourself anything, i.e. love, acceptance, reassurance, forgiveness, a hug?
    What does being Below-Zero mean to you now?

    Alternatively…

13. **Do you know anyone who has been here?**
    What was it like for them?
    What was it like for you?
    What does Below-Zero mean to you now?

9. Climbing Back in the Window

As demonstrated throughout this book, staying within the window is more ideal than leaving and having to get back in from the outside. However, life is life. Shit happens. Life happens. We can never expect anyone to live a life where they do not enter survival mode ever again, because that might be exactly what is needed of them. For example, next time they have to move out of the way of a bus in a hurry. There are a multitude of things that can and do happen, in a normal life, with real risks, losses, heartbreaks, and threats, around us.

Once safety is restored, and knowing what we do about the effects on functioning, getting back into the window, becomes the very next priority. Here you can access more adequate cognitive functioning, and the other steps forward are more easily executed.

Resistance or Self-Preservation

Before we start climbing back in, it would first pay to visit a therapist's favorite little friend, resistance. If you have noticed any internal resistance to the concept of living your life back within the window, or at a calmer, healthier level, that is not unheard of. It is totally understandable. When you have been living out of the window for some time, the concept of living within it may be foreign to you and can be associated with scary things, like vulnerability. Or perhaps some idea in our mind of 'what it is to be a man', or that to have worth we must always be busy.

"How ever will you survive?" a flustered inner voice may query, imagining a place without your 'hyper-alertness', and other defense mechanisms to 'keep you safe'. Perhaps being back within the window is associated with weakness or whatever event/s happened, to make you leave it in the first place. This makes total sense. Especially if the world you have known, has not been a safe or comfortable place to be. Living in the window is a very different place from what has become the norm for you. Give yourself time. This work is a journey and adventure, not a one-stop, instant teleportation to some ideal destination.

Climbing Back in the Window

We have to remember that our survival modes are all there for a reason. We need to make sure our current environment is safe before we can be expected to de-escalate... otherwise of course we will meet resistance within. It wouldn't be 'resistance', in the term I refer to though. It would be your inner wisdom — Your self-preservation mechanism trying to keep you safe. We must first find out whether we are in this state because of past factors or ones posing a current threat. Sometimes it can be tricky to figure out. It could be a combination of the two.

(Sadly, this is a confusion that is taken advantage of by predators when 'grooming' an individual, or seeking to manipulate someone to go against their higher wisdom, for their own gain. A bit of a tangent but thought I'd throw that in there. Get familiar with your inner voice and honor it.)

Having a small 'break' from survival mode may allow you to figure this out. A break from the current environment too perhaps. Continue reading. The following 'De-escalation - First Aid' should help. Giving you some calm in which you can access the rational part of your brain, to decipher these questions better. Your inner guidance will speak clearly at lower levels of the window too. If not clearer.

Climbing Back in the Window

If you remain currently in a hostile environment that triggers your survival instincts, then you need to address this before you can expect to be able to live a calm, regulated life. It is not fair to expect someone to function within their window while existing in an abusive, neglectful, or otherwise unsafe situation. Instead, survival modes should be engaged in a useful way that motivates you to restore your safety. If this applies to you, what boundaries do you need to implement to restore your sense of safety?

Resistance may also arise from the assumption it will be boring in the window since you have become accustomed to hyperstimulated states. As we've acknowledged, some people choose to live outside the window for a reason. We might only be confronted by this element for us, once we commence our journey back inside it, and notice we are 'digging our heels in' in resistance.

There could be several contributing factors to resistance to change. I would recommend Checking-In and journaling, to unpack as much of this as you need. Potentially there is work that is best done with a Therapist. However, do continue through the rest of the book if you can. Even getting this far shows a strong inclination for change. You will already have developed some good insights propelling you down this path. You're almost there. At the very least, you can still 'choose' to stay outside the window and that is totally up to you.

Mindfulness and Body

We discussed earlier the 'Brain and Body' connection, and now we are briefly reflecting on the 'Mind and Body' connection. That being, the intentional use of the mind — Mindfulness.

To recap; the body can sometimes 'trick' the brain into thinking something is wrong. The brain tries to 'justify' why the body is chemically in Fight/Flight, stimulated, rapid heart rate, etc. "There must be a threat," it says and then makes stuff up about what the threat is.

Well, we can use this same connection for good. By relaxing, calming, and de-escalating our body, our brain soon follows. And vice versa. Because they are so connected, any message from one to the other has the potential to spiral and amplify. In this case, we WANT this to happen. We want to be happy, and only highly reactionary when physically necessary. When safety calls for it.

The brain is a series of physical connections and links, but I refer to the mind as the thing that directs the brain. Something other than the physical. Usually discussed in Eastern Philosophy because Western paradigms don't have much science on it.

The following exercises of the book employ an element of this effect. Optimizing your change-making capabilities by getting the mind, brain, and body together on the same side. On YOUR side.

You can 'trick' your brain into believing just about anything, so make it good stuff that serves you. Not the other way around.

De-escalation - First Aid

This is a helpful exercise that can be used to 'ground' yourself when feeling heightened or outside of your window. An excellent 'first-aid' to restore an initial amount of equilibrium, before embarking on other steps. Here I have listed some of my favorite techniques that can easily be used anywhere, to restore calm and functioning, or even just for a little self-love top-up. Used as an entire sequence or on their own, these techniques can serve as initial steps before engaging in activities like the 'Check-In' exercise or utilizing other resources provided in this book. As usual, make them your own, be creative, tune in to yourself, freestyle it. Do what feels good in the moment.

1. **Take a slow, deep breath.** Take another. Slow it down. Take as many slow, deep breaths as you need. The power of breathing for regulating the nervous system and restoring brain functioning is so underrated. This should be your 'go-to' first step. Sometimes on its own, it can be enough to calm you sufficiently.
2. **Relax your jaw.** This act alone has a ripple effect on your entire nervous system. Did you notice you relaxed your shoulders too?
3. **Wriggle your toes.** Wriggle your fingers. Rub your hands together or rub your hands on your thighs. This act of 'grounding' can also be seen as being closer to 'ground 0'. As escalation occurs, we tend to become more caught up in our thoughts, be 'all up in our head' or 'have our head in the clouds', and less attuned to our bodily sensations. Therefore, practices that help reconnect us with our physical presence, bringing us mentally back into the moment, and back down the window.
4. **Hug yourself.** Wrap your arms around yourself at your chest and rub the top of your arms, like a warm loving hug. Go on, do it now. The

neuroscience behind this simple act is phenomenal, especially due to the added benefits of the bilateral stimulation on each side of the body. Not something I'll elaborate on here. Just enjoy it and use it often.

5. **Do a little 'Check In'** with yourself. Close your eyes and Check-In. What are your needs right now? What are your factors?
Either a mini one on the spot, or a more in-depth working through of the exercise when you have time. This can help to identify what factors have triggered this escalation so you can have a more effective overall address of your situation and the elements leading to it. You may even find that after a good de-escalation, those things bothering you weren't really worth the energy. We see things from quite a different perspective further down the window.

There are quite a lot of good De-escalation and Grounding techniques out there. The '5 senses game' is a good one. A lot of the activities we mention soon in 'resiliency factors' can also help to de-escalate in the moment too. Initially, however, it's good to have these simple steps you can do right away, anywhere, anytime, without too much brain power.

Addressing your Factors

As you can tell, we are now delving into the 'What do I do about it' part of the book. When previously discussing toxic positivity, we emphasized that ignoring or dismissing underlying factors only postpones the issues and prolongs their suffering of them. It's crucial to confront and address these factors to be able to live a life free from unnecessary stress and trauma. In the following activity, we take a deeper exploration into the factors that contribute to your position in the Window of Tolerance, and with self-awareness and strategy start to carefully address them.

Activity. 6 - Factors: Address or Mitigate

The question is, what factors do I ...

- Get rid of completely
- Reduce in severity
- Change somehow
- Or Mitigate with additional resiliency factors.

The Serenity Prayer comes to mind here; have the courage to change the things you can, the serenity to accept the things you can not change, and the wisdom to know the difference.

Climbing Back in the Window

Let's apply the multiple window perspective for this one...

1. You can **go back to your 'House of Windows' (Activity, 3)**, and make notes on it, draw up another one... or you can just reflect. Make sure it includes all the factors that currently pertain to you but as their own window.

2. How **many windows are over a level 7?** You might want to highlight these somehow.

3. **Are there some that need dialing down a bit?** Is this an easy task? Is changing your perspective on these windows enough? What else needs to happen?

4. **Are there others that you may be able to utilize more for support**; untapped resources as such?

5. **Are there some areas of life that are a bit messy and could be compartmentalized a bit more**, i.e. parts that need their own window?
Are there areas of life taking up too much room on your main window, when actually, they are just their own window over there?

6. **Do these situations need some 'Boundaries'** between them in which to bring some separation? Or is it enough for you just to compartmentalize them in your thinking?

7. **What behaviors could you start adopting** in which to implement boundaries, or to manage these windows better in general?

8. **What Tools or resiliency factors could you bring in to make some windows bigger and give you more room?**

9. **Are there any that you could just cross right off?** Things you don't have any control over or aren't yours to worry about? Other people's concerns you've taken on or fears that have no probability? If you can't completely scratch them out now, is this a longer-term goal? How can you lower the rating on these? Make notes.

10. **What other changes can you make to 'get back in the window'?** (Something we will explore more in the following activity).

Building Resiliency

Your reading so far has already begun building on your resiliency. You have

- Improved self-awareness
- Learned how to monitor yourself
- Improved your self-therapy toolkit
- Studied your pre-existing resiliency factors
- Come up with more of your own de-escalation and resilience ideas
- And, through the process of formulating your own answers and ideas, you've likely developed greater confidence in your abilities as well.

This boosting of self-efficacy is a huge resiliency factor in itself. Stepping into your own power and being your own hero is an overall goal of our work here. You ARE your own hero. You are your own expert and YOU are your own answer. Living in this knowledge, is a powerhouse of resiliency already.

Resiliency Building is not only about 'First Aid' immediate relief techniques and mitigating factors that have gotten out of hand. It is about creating a life that you don't want to escape from. By integrating the following tools into your daily, weekly, and monthly routines, you're creating a stronger foundation for navigating life's inevitable fluctuations. This allows you to more easily bounce back inside the window when escalations happen.

Activity. 7 - Your Resiliency Factors

In previous activities, we have thoroughly examined and addressed our stress factors. We are now listing our resiliency factors in a similar way. Finally, we're getting to the sweet stuff, the 'icing on the cake'. Good on you for making it this far and doing the hard work cleaning out the closet. Give yourself a hug and say thank you.

1. This is the good stuff. We want to be exploring, investigating, and indulging in our resiliency factors. We want this to be big, beautiful, and abundant, so give yourself plenty of room and creative permission. **You can list or draw these as a mind map. Do a painting, collage, or vision board, whatever makes you feel awesome.** This is your 'go to' page when you need it.

2. First, **add to this page all the resiliency factors you have already come up with** in previous activities and reflections. If you have found this book helpful, you could add that in

there too. As we go through the following list add the ideas and inspirations that suit you.

3. Next, we're thinking of **things we can do in the moment, like the De-escalation First Aid** exercise above. What other ideas do you have that can help you bring your rating down when you first notice it going up?

4. **Who can you talk to?** Who are the people on your Resiliency Team? Different people might offer different kinds of support, but all are valid. Talking is a huge mitigation of stress factors. Together we are so much stronger. Don't try to be an island. You are not a rock. You have a heartbeat. Honor your humanness and need for connection.

5. We spoke of grounding earlier. If you can, **get outside, or better yet in nature**. This seems to help immensely. Try it with babies and small children when they are having a meltdown. They know what's up. In our modern lives, we do not 'ground' ourselves enough. There is something about being out in the sounds and sights of nature that seems to 'rewire' us back to a default setting. I don't even know if that is Evidence-Based / scientific or not, but I'll put

my name down as saying there is something primally healing about being in nature.

6. **Take care of your health, fitness, and physical well-being**. Mind and body connection being what it is, this is super important. I know it's a bit cliche and some are sick of hearing it, especially when you are in a low-functioning place in the window. Sometimes 'doing' anything other than the necessities feels like just another stressor. If you can, make exercise and good nutrition something you enjoy. The Gym isn't for everyone. What about a walk on the beach or in the bush? A YouTube yoga class in the morning? Have a lounge disco. Whatever it is that works for you, gets you moving.

    Looking into nutrition and deficiency is also important if you feel this may be a factor for you. Stress chews through your B vitamin stores. Magnesium supplements can also be extremely helpful for some people presenting with anxiety symptoms. I highly recommend looking into this side of things, if you feel you may be lacking in something.

7. **Mindfulness practices**. Meditation, affirmation, yoga, listening to guided relaxations on YouTube or Spotify. Doing a class in your area in any of these sorts of things.

Applying mindfulness (being mindfully, immersed in the moment) to everyday tasks is a helpful mindset in itself.

8. **Reading, listening to, or watching inspirational content.** Be careful what brain food you are consuming. If it's depressing or upsetting, notice how it affects your placement on the window. The right song, Netflix series, or book can be life-changing. What are some that you could start to incorporate into your life?

9. **Sensory Input.** This is a great one to explore. The right sensory input can be hugely comforting and de-escalating. These things can help to be grounding, bring you back into your body, and tell your nervous system it's a pleasant, safe place to be. Think scented candles, aromatherapy, fluffy cushions, dim lighting, soft or uplifting music, tasty or textural food, hot baths, and the sounds of birds and waterfalls. What are your favorite smells, textures, sounds, sights, tastes, temperatures? There are no wrong answers.

10. **Places and activities**. Having discussed the power of sensory input you can see why places like the Beach and Forest are so healing for

people. What are your favorite places and things to do? What were they in the past? Why did you stop doing them and what can you do now to get that same benefit back? Are there things you've always wanted to do or places you've wanted to go? What's stopping you?

11. **Go back to the prompts in Activity. 1** and what can be inspired from there. What **internal resiliency factors**; skills, and strengths do you have? **External**; work, material, lifestyle? **Generational? Societal?** There is so much to be grateful for when we look at some of these bigger-picture privileges we have in many parts of the developed world. We have rights, resources, and protective factors many people don't. What parts of your community and society are a form of support, security, and resiliency to you? What could you utilize more?

10. How to Stay in Your Window

When 'Tools' Become Resilience

Sustainable change is not just a practice, but making it your lifestyle. Using therapeutic and self-care tools regularly is where they start to become resiliency factors, not just getting you back in the window but helping you stay there. Whether you adopt suggestions from this book or devise your own strategies, routinely integrating these practices into your lifestyle, so they become a normalized way of being, is the basis for living a life well, within your Window of Tolerance.

By road mapping, like we have through this book, and building our self-awareness, we have a good idea by now, of how to keep all our windows in good condition. We know our factors and triggers, the ones we need to watch out for, and what to do to manage them when things get out of control. You will continue to get better at this the more you do it.

Now, when escalating up your Window of Tolerance, you will catch yourself at an 8 and do what you need to de-escalate. Then when that gets easy, you will catch yourself at a 6. Before now... when did you catch yourself? Was it after you had hurt someone else? When you were about to face a negative consequence to your Fight or Flight behavior? Was it 3 days later when your brain had calmed enough to reflect clearly? Did you catch yourself at all? Or just free fall from there into depression? This can all change.

Like anything, starting is the hardest part. Making new neuro-pathways for changed behaviors is like cutting a new track through a bush. It's way easier to just walk the trodden path that's been trampled a thousand times before. Cutting a new path can feel like hacking through scrub with a machete. At times you may want to give up or think there is no end because you can't see it yet. You will probably feel a little lost for much of this time and question if you are doing the right thing. The first time will be the hardest. Then the second time is easier, and before you know it, this is the easiest path, the default one. You just walk it mindlessly, at speed, while the other track is grown over and barely distinguishable anymore.

Do you remember learning to drive? It felt so 'clunky'. Every action had to pass through the frontal cortex of your brain and be intentional and considered. Hands, arms, and eyes going everywhere at once. "Do this, look there, don't forget to take that off, put that on, not too much". Who didn't hit a crisis point either learning to drive or teaching someone else? Now you probably hop in the car, turn up at your destination, and forget how you even got there. All those little actions have become so automated, it all happens in the cerebellum at the back of your head and you only use the front of your head to keep your sunglasses on.

Managing your life and staying within your Window of Tolerance will become like this.

Boundaries

A discussion on 'How to stay in your window' would not be complete without a mention of Boundaries. They are going to be the things that protect your new rhythm within your window. Having already touched on these briefly while 'Addressing our factors', and separating one window into many, it is easy to see why the use of Boundaries is so beneficial.

Many people may benefit from you being out of your window, or close to it. Your boss may have come to expect your over-commitment at work. Your drug dealer may not want to lose their greatest customer.

Your 'friends' may not want to lose their 'Party Partner'. Even a parent may benefit from you being in a state of anxiousness or low functioning if it increases your dependency on them and means you won't leave them.

There are all sorts of ways our windows interact with other people's windows. I could write a book on this alone… another day. Here we just need to know that what we want in our interactions is a mutually beneficial influence. Unfortunately, what we can get when our windows are edging out, is an opportunity for others to take advantage or manipulate us.

We may also form codependency, where we equally get something from the dysfunctional connection too. Trauma bonds are an example of playing out your negative programming with each other in some odd, unspoken agreement. This unhealthy form of connection usually happens at extreme ends of the window, sometimes going between above and below. If you could map it, it would look very much like enmeshed, intertwined lifelines, because that's exactly how it is, bounding the other to each other and not in a good way. Nestled safely within your window, you don't usually have the same 'neediness', nor vulnerability to other people's manipulation.

How to Stay in Your Window

If we are looking to change our ways and behaviors that keep us in a shitty part of our window, we are going to have to have boundaries with these people and situations in our life. We will need boundaries with anything that seeks to influence us away from healthy functioning.

Asserting your boundaries means communicating them, and then also backing that communication with action where needed. Doing what you need, to protect your new level within the window and your new behavior and practices that keep you there. That may mean physical separation. Sometimes it means a Restraining Order.

You don't ever have to apologize to anyone else for doing what is loving and caring for yourself. Ultimately what is right for you, is right for others. Your boundaries can serve as a mirror in which they can reflect, truly see themselves, and learn about their own lives. If they take this opportunity, or just waste it on blame and avoidance, to stay in their maladaptive behavioral loops, then that's completely on them. You can still love someone, from all the distance you need to protect yourself. You can still send them well wishes from a place in the window where they may not be able to get to, or where they can not get the same things out of you.

As mentioned, interacting with other people's windows and 'looking through' other people's windows, to better understand them, is a whole book of its own. For now, being aware of your need for boundaries, communicating/implementing them however you need, and protecting your place in YOUR window, is enough.

What the Fuck is Right With Me?

When we are at levels 0-5, we do not ask "What the fuck is wrong with me?", we are saying "Wow, look at how much is right with me!"

The voice that comes through now is the echo of your inner Parent. The grown-up, that gazes lovingly at your inner child and sees the perfection of such an adorable, learning, mistake-making, wonder. For a life in the window, this love becomes the standard. The default setting. Of course, you are loved and lovable. Of course, you are good enough. It is the unquestioned assumption. The absence of doubt, which forms cracks in this knowledge. It is the realization that whatever countered this, was not 'of you', nor ever real at all.

So I guess, we are going to talk about "What the fuck is right with Suzy" after all....And if I was to surmise, I'd say she was loved... And so kept loving herself.

Activity. 8 - Light It Up

Use this gem in abundance! Do it often. Do mini versions throughout the day. Do intensive versions on waking and before sleeping. Do them on the bus, in a plane, on a train...you get the aim.

It will lift your vibe and help familiarize your neurology with being relaxed, happy, and safe. Strengthening those neuro-pathways to become the dominant ones. This is a great exercise to follow up the Check-in or the De-escalation - First Aid too. It is also a great activity to wrap up our work.

What a brave step you have taken, even picking this book up. Getting past the confronting title and casting honest eyes upon your life. Although this is not always easy. A process that can see us reliving old hurts, as we dig through emotional closets to declutter, we also find those gems within us along the way. The things we want to dust off and keep.... treasure and protect.

1. **Optional: If you can, first create a space** where you are comfortable and won't be

disturbed. This will help to get the most out of this practice. Set a scene if you like. Keeping in mind the sensory resiliency factors we talked about earlier, you can use candles, cushions, and whatever symbolistic objects pertain to you and your beliefs, to do this.

Although, as mentioned, you can do a mini version of this activity just about anywhere, keep in mind that the full version here can create a euphoric type state and wouldn't be safe to do while operating a vehicle or where your full attention is needed elsewhere. Commonsense should be applied to all activities in this book.

2. **Let's now 'Check In' with ourselves**. Take a few slow deep breaths, close your eyes if it helps, and try to locate an area within your body that feels good.

3. Alternatively, you can try to **remember a time you felt good / safe / happy.** Imagine being there again. What was happening around you? How did you feel? And go from there.

4. **Notice where in your body that good feeling is and just observe it.**

5. What is its temperature? What color is it? What shape is it? What texture? What softness is it?

6. **Sit with that feeling and let it emanate like a light outwards over your body.** Let it flow and expand over your neck and head, out through your arms to your fingertips, and down through your legs and toes. Flushing away any tension or blockages along that way.

7. **Notice your whole body relax** and adjust to this increasing level of lightness. Releasing and relaxing more and more.

8. Is there anywhere that is a challenge for this sensation to go? Does it need more focus and attention to move there? Lovingly query as to what is going on there and **observe without judgment, any sensations, hints, or feelings.** Then let it go and release the area even more.

9. **Feel this sensation move outwards from your body to also fill the space around your body.** Let it flow and grow as it needs and just observe without judgment as it does.

10. When you get well practiced at this you can begin to **expand this love and light further outward if you want to.** You can send it out to

any area you like, your whole home and property. Send it to loved ones. Let it dissolve tension and blockages and anything it needs along the way.

11. Sit with that ever-amplifying light and relax as long as you like and then **when you are done, feel the light draw back into your body and contain it there**. Encapsulated within your heart and soul.

12. **Become aware of your breath again and very slowly come back to your surroundings.** Do things to help you **ground.** Rub your hands together. Wriggle your toes. Rub the soles of your feet on the ground. Drink a glass of water. Get outside and have a walk in the garden or something similar if you feel like it.

13. Know that this beautiful 'place' and light, exists within you, to access at any time. **This light is you and of you.** It is the place that knows your worth and loves to love you, without question. Let this light shine always and remind you of your truth and what peaceful power you are capable of. Know in the future when things don't align with this calm, loved, and lighter version of you, or seek to disrupt or compromise it, rather than add to it, if

How to Stay in Your Window

something feels off, you have full permission to utilize assertiveness and boundaries to feel back in connection with that safe space again

11. Conclusion

Well done. You made it, to the end of this book, yet perhaps only the beginning of a lifelong self-explorative adventure. Throughout this book, we've scanned the complexities of the human experience, delved into the depths of our emotions, and navigated the twists and turns of our inner landscapes.

At the heart of our exploration lies the concept of the Window of Tolerance – that balance between arousal and regulation, where we find ourselves able to manage life's challenges with self-awareness and resilience. We've learned that being outside this window can manifest in various ways, from overwhelming anxiety to numbing dissociation, and that recognizing these signs is the first step towards reclaiming our equilibrium.

By understanding the dynamics of our Window of Tolerance, we've gained insight into our patterns of behavior, our reactions to stressors, and the ways in which we can cultivate greater emotional regulation and resilience. We've discovered the power of mindfulness, self-awareness, and self-compassion as tools for traversing the highs and lows of our

Conclusion

emotional landscape and finding our way back to center.

But perhaps most importantly, we've come to realize that there is nothing inherently wrong with us. We are human, with all the complexities, contradictions, and imperfections that come with it. Our struggles do not define us; rather, they are an integral part of our journey toward self-love, mastery, and growth.

As we close this book, let us carry with us the wisdom gained from our exploration of self. Let us remember that we have the power to regulate our emotions, conquer life's challenges, and cultivate resilience in the face of adversity. And let us embrace the journey of self-discovery with courage, compassion, and curiosity.

So, "What the fuck is wrong with me?" Nothing. Absolutely nothing. We are simply human, imperfect, and beautifully flawed. There is no end destination or 'precipice of perfection'. We just get better at the ride.

Thank you for joining me on this journey. May you continue to explore, grow, and thrive, within the ever-expanding boundaries of your own Window of Tolerance.

Conclusion

Love Mel

www.ingramcontent.com/pod-product-compliance
Lightning Source LLC
Chambersburg PA
CBHW020805160426
43192CB00006B/455